PASTORAL MINI

PASTORAL MINISTRY FOR TODAY

'Who Do You Say That I Am?'

Conference Papers 2008

Edited by Thomas G. Grenham

VERITAS

First published 2009 by
Veritas Publications
7/8 Lower Abbey Street
Dublin 1
Ireland
Email publications@veritas.ie
Website www.veritas.ie

ISBN 978 1 84730 173 4

10 9 8 7 6 5 4 3 2 1

A catalogue record for this book is available from the British Library.

Cover design by Niamh McGarry
Typesetting by Barbara Croatto
Printed in the Republic of Ireland by ColourBooks Ltd, Dublin

Veritas books are printed on paper made from the wood pulp of managed forests.
For every tree felled, at least one tree is planted, thereby renewing natural resources.

CHALLENGES AND
OPPORTUNITIES FOR MINISTRY

Most Rev. Diarmuid Martin
Archbishop of Dublin and Primate of Ireland

I am pleased to be here at the opening of this conference on Pastoral Ministry [November 2008] which takes as its overarching theme the question asked by Jesus in St Mark's Gospel: 'Who do you say that I am?' (Mk 8:29)

For most of the month of October I was in Rome attending the XII Ordinary General Assembly of the Synod of Bishops on the theme of 'The Word of God in the Life and Mission of the Church'. It was an interesting occasion, described to me by one bishop as an act of reception on the Dogmatic Constitution *Dei Verbum* on Revelation, which has in many ways been a poor relative among the documents of the Vatican Council. The Roman Catholic Church has a long way to go to re-discover the centrality of the Word of God in its own life and as the great treasure we share with our brothers and sisters of other Christian denominations. I look forward to seeing how we can intensify our biblical apostolate in the Archdiocese of Dublin in the years to come.

One of the very practical pastoral reminders that was brought home to me listening to the over 200 interventions of bishops from around the world during the Synod was that you should be careful about using short excerpts from the scriptures, taken outside their context in the scripture and away from the context from which they emerged. So I was left a little uneasy about simply referring to the short scriptural text which was presented in the title of the conference, and felt that I must turn back to St Mark's Gospel to see in a little more detail what the text is about and what its context is.

The context opens out many interesting aspects of the text which are relevant to our theme. I can only presume that this was indeed obvious to the scholars who prepared the conference and chose the text, but allow me, not as a scripture scholar but as one with responsibility for the renewal of pastoral thrust in a populous and diverse diocese, to trace out my own reflections around that text as you begin your two days.

If we look at Mark 8, we see first of all that the question 'who do you say that I am?' is the follow-up to another question 'Who do people say that I am?' This seems to be saying that one should expect a difference in the quality of answer about the identity of Jesus on the part of those who are called to be his more intimate disciples, as opposed to the well-intentioned bystanders or what we might today call the general public.

But the matter turns out to be not quite so simple. Many people at the time of Jesus had heard about him, had seen him, had heard something about his words and his actions. The question about 'who he was' was being asked by many, with varying responses and varying motivation. The reaction of some is hostility and rejection. Others, like those from his own home town, felt that they knew all about him and his family anyway. Paradoxically, that information – in itself totally correct – became an obstacle to them recognising Jesus' true identity. There were also many who were puzzled by his identity but who began to look towards him – in this case incorrectly – as perhaps the reappearance of some powerful figure of the Old Testament, or as a precursor of something important to come.

Curiously, the incontestable facts, which the inhabitants of his own home town had and which led them away from his identity, and the reappearance of the incorrect conclusions of those who thought him a prophet may in fact have been the beginnings of an attitude which is open to faith, even if the content of that faith is as yet still unclear.

The question becomes even more complex. Jesus now turns to his close followers and asks them who they say he is. The response of Peter is of such correctness that it would seem to satisfy even the most exacting professor: Peter proclaims: 'You are the Christ.' Yet curiously this reply does not elicit an overenthusiastic reaction on the part of Jesus. In the Gospel of Mark, Jesus simply warns them not to talk to anyone about this.

Here again we see that many of our black and white answers about where we begin to encounter Jesus in his true identity are inadequate. The people who are puzzled about Jesus' identity and come to apparently wrong conclusions, at least show that they do have some idea as to where they should be looking to understand who Jesus is and how his identity and mission can be understood. They do so by reference to the great figures who appear along the path of God's dealing with his people. They look to those who along the path of the history of salvation purified faith from the many incursions of false Gods which had defiled faith in their history – a phenomenon which continues also in our contemporary society.

The apparently correct answer of Peter, on the other hand, turns out also to be an imperfect answer, since effectively while Peter appears to recognise Jesus as the Christ, his understanding of who the Christ was to be was far from the truth. Immediately after asking this question, Jesus begins to reveal dimensions of his own identity and mission which Peter cannot accept. Jesus begins to talk of a Messiah whose identity would be revealed in rejection and violent death. Peter's response reveals itself shortly afterwards, despite its apparent correctness, to be more the vision of Satan than of God.

The disciples who heard the question 'who do you say that I am' thought they had it definitively right. Jesus' questioning was however only the beginnings of a process which would indeed take the disciples on a path they never imagined and found hard to accept. Jesus teaching was such as to turn their understanding of God and of Jesus head over heels. Jesus' revelation about himself shocks them and only very slowly do they begin to realise that they must open their minds and their hearts; in such a way, not just their minds but their whole way of life was about to be changed and turned head over heels.

Our topic is pastoral theology. It is about a theology able to reach out and challenge all of us about our understanding of the identity of Jesus and how that challenge affects the way we live as individuals and as the Church, the community of the followers of Jesus in the realities of today.

The first thing we have to stress then is that the response we are talking about is not something of our own construction. It comes from the self-revelation of God who appears in Jesus Christ as a God who loves us with an infinite gratuitousness. On our own we can never totally fathom such a love. It is a self-giving love which will never allow us to be smug and self-satisfied about our fully knowing of who Jesus is. It is a love that challenges us day by day in the deeper manner to be gripped in our being by the person and the life of Jesus himself.

Like Peter who gives what appears to be a perfectly correct answer, all forms of self-defined correctness may lead us completely astray in our seeking of Jesus, while some of the less correct searching of contemporary bystanders may well be a sign of a sincere, positive openness and beginning of the road to true faith.

Faith has to be inculturated and inserted into the particular realities of the times and we need to have a precise and accurate idea of what those realities are. The face of belief in Ireland is changing and we have to admit that for one of the most catechised populations of all Europe, if you think in terms of the period of religious education that our young people receive right throughout their primary and secondary education, there is no way we can feel smug about the situation of faith in our midst.

Statistics are useful but may be misleading. The indications recently gathered about religious practice in the Archdiocese of Dublin seem to show that practice on an average Sunday is below 20 per cent of the population and that over the past three years there has been a drop of about 11 per cent. Mass attendance on its own is not an all-embracing criterion to estimate people's religious adherence or the level of their faith. Many attend religious service on a regular but not weekly basis. Others who might never attend

Church still remain religious persons and are indeed good people, full of ideals and commitment and care for others, whose faith is not adequately explicated yet certainly not absent. Indeed, it is possible that those with inadequate answers may be closer on the path to faith than those who can recite all the right answers but whose understanding of faith is miles wide of what true faith is.

I am struck by the many people I encounter whose faith is not the joyful and free response to the message of a God who loves us, but one which is fearful and insecure and full of anxieties. On the other hand, there are others whose faith and lifestyle are marked by an arrogance and self-assertiveness which is far from the simplicity and lovingness which must be a mark of the believer in Jesus.

Faith must be inculturated, but faith must also be de-culturated; it must always have that freshness which allows it to challenge the underlying cultural values of any age in the light of the Gospel, also in areas that will make us unpopular and even experience rejection and ridicule. Every culture is invaded by false Gods which distort and defile true faith.

Every culture and every generation can fall prey to superficial human reflection which projects as good what may be a long way from how reality is seen by the eyes of God. Each culture can bring newness but each culture can be like that factual knowledge of Jesus' own townsfolk and can actually be a hindrance to understanding Jesus.

The Synod on the Word of God, in its final message, refers to the Church as 'The House of the Word'. Pastoral theology must be a realisation of that reality, the Church as the place where the Word is preached, broken and accepted, especially in the context of the Breaking of the Bread and in a spirit of prayer and brotherly love.

CONTENTS

CONTRIBUTORS

Thomas G. Grenham SPS, Ph.D., is the Associate Dean for Student Affairs and Head of the Department of Pastoral Theology at the Milltown Institute, Dublin. He teaches courses on pastoral/practical theology, mission theology and ministry. He has broad experience in ministry, having worked in many parishes in different parts of the world. A member of St Patrick's Missionary Society, Kiltegan, Co. Wicklow, he served as a missionary for many years among the Turkana of Kenya. He received his interdisciplinary Ph.D. in theology and education from Boston College, Massachusetts, in 2002 and a Masters in Pastoral Ministry at the same university. His publications include *The Unknown God: Religious and Theological Interculturation* (Peter Lang, 2005).

Timothy Radcliffe OP was born in London in 1945. He joined the English Province of the Dominican Order in 1965, and was ordained a priest in 1971. He studied at Blackfriars and at St John's College in Oxford, and in Paris. He was a chaplain to the University of London from 1974–76, before returning to Oxford, where he taught scripture and doctrine for twelve years. Besides teaching and preaching, he was involved in the peace movement and in ministry to people with AIDS. He was Prior of Oxford from 1982–88, when he was elected Provincial of the English Province. He was President of the Conference of Major Religious Superiors. In 1992 he was elected Master of the Order, finishing his term in 2001. He was Chancellor of the Angelicum University in Rome, S.Tomas in Manila, the École Biblique in Jerusalem and the Theology Faculty in Fribourg. He is now an itinerant preacher and lecturer, based at Blackfriars, Oxford, spending two-thirds of the year travelling, and is on the board of the Catholic Agency for Overseas Development. In 2007 he was awarded the Michael Ramsey Prize for theological writing, and his most recent book is *Why Go to Church?* (Continuum, 2008).

Michael Carroll, Ph.D., is a Fellow of the British Association for Counselling and Psychotherapy, a chartered counselling psychologist and a BACP senior registered practitioner. He is an accredited executive coach and an accredited supervisor of executive coaches with the Association for Professional Executive Coaches and Supervisors. He is also Visiting Industrial Professor in the Graduate School of Education, University of Bristol. In 2001 Michael was the winner of the British Psychological Society Award for Distinguished Contributions to Professional Psychology. His books include *Integrative Approaches to Supervision* (edited with Margaret Tholstrup, 2001); *On Being a Supervisee: Creating Learning Partnerships* (with Maria Gilbert, 2005); and *Becoming an Executive Coachee* (with Maria Gilbert, 2008).

Anne Codd PBVM, Ph.D., a native of Wexford, is a Presentation Sister. She currently works as resource person for the Irish Catholic Bishops' Commission for Pastoral Renewal and Adult Faith Development. Anne's undergraduate studies in science and theology paved the way for an abiding interest in a Living Systems approach to social, educational and ecclesial contexts. Having ministered for fifteen years in secondary-level schools in Ireland and the UK, Anne pursued her graduate studies at the University of Liverpool, focusing on the school as an agent of learning in the community. During her subsequent ten years in parish ministry she brought her pastoral practice into dialogue with theology at Trinity College, Dublin, where she completed her doctoral thesis on 'Church as Community, Theological Foundations and Development in Practice'. As she moved to the field of pastoral training, Anne became increasingly convinced that didactic approaches alone do not foster transformation, and so she joined a training group in consultancy and facilitation at the Craighead Institute, Glasgow. There she enjoyed and appreciated the combination of Ignatian perspectives on organisations combined with human-relations and open-systems approaches to development.

Bairbre de Búrca is a mother and grandmother and lives in the parish of Balally, Co. Dublin. She has over forty years of experience of living in that parish and continues to be an active participant in both parish and community life. She was involved in the introduction of the Parish Development and Renewal programme (PDR) in Balally. She served as a member of Bishop Donal Murray's area team for PDR and subsequently was nominated as a diocesan representative on the Bishops' Commission for the Laity. Bairbre has practiced for many years as a psychosynthesis psychotherapist in Eckhart House, Dublin. She is a member of the Irish Association of Humanistic and Integrative Psychotherapy (IAHIP). She holds a diploma in Adult and Continuing Education from NUI Maynooth and a Masters degree in Pastoral Leadership from All Hallows College, Dublin. Among her many professional roles within the area of pastoral ministry, she taught on the Family Studies Programme at Marino Institute of Education, Dublin. She is currently chaplain to the students and staff of the Milltown Institute, Dublin.

WHO DO YOU SAY THAT I AM?

Thomas G. Grenham

This book is a compilation of papers delivered at the pastoral conference organised by the Pastoral Theology Department of the Milltown Institute of Theology and Philosophy, Dublin, in November 2008. The papers presented were the fruit of the reflections of four speakers. The last chapter is a specially solicited chapter from a participant at the conference to provide readers with some reflections and proposals for doing theology and ministry in the future. The title of the conference, 'Who Do You Say That I Am?', became the foundation question in the exploration of contemporary pastoral theology and ministry, a question that Jesus asked of his disciples. Jesus wanted to know from them what they and others were thinking about his identity and sense of ministry. This book is about exploring that question.

Ministry is, in many ways, about that question. It is a crucial question in the discovery of a life-giving and meaningful pastoral theology with its challenges and opportunities for ministry in today's world. The way Jesus ministered in the world of his day was dependent on the evolving sense of his own self in dialogue with the notion of who God was for him. The question 'Who do you say that I am?' was about reading the signs of the times in Jesus' historical era. Some of these signs included cultural taboos, marginalisation of the poor, religious sectarianism/inclusivism, gender inequality, political struggle, racism and suspicion of the stranger. These issues also resonate in our own time. Comprehending the signs, amidst the diversity of cultures and religions in which our identity, in particular our pastoral identity, is shaped, provides markers for effective ministry. For example, how we use language to articulate our deepest feelings and thoughts and the ways in which we decode symbols, rituals and customs to reveal life-giving meaning is challenging for ministers in a multicultural environment. Understanding the signs reflected in values, attitudes and perceptions as well as comprehending the codes of society, politics, economics and religion generally can be difficult. To communicate and disseminate these signs into relevant meaning for the world is at the core of the development of a practical theology. Practical theology gives life and hope to relevant ministry. Practical theologian Terry Veling says that:

> To read the signs of the times is one of the most difficult theological tasks, yet it is a theological imperative. Too often we do not behold the announcement of God in our present reality. Rather, we cling to what we already know of God, to tired and weary theological frameworks that have lost their sense of timeliness, to religious truths that lull us to sleep rather than provoke us to wakefulness.[1]

The world around us and the diversity of the faith traditions to which we belong shape us in our personhood. It is hoped that this book will assist readers in weaving a life-giving pastoral theology in order to live and work effectively with post-modern uncertainty. The insights presented in this book will help provide opportunities for personal and communal reflection on ministry in contemporary Ireland and beyond. The material will help the reader to engage, reflect and re-imagine their sense of identity in ministry. Readers will find practical hints and suggestions to sustain and foster quality and effectiveness in their task of doing everyday caring ministry.

Given today's general global and local fragmentation, exacerbated currently by the continuing uncertainty around the world financial system, it is opportune for readers to focus on uncovering the intercultural face of God emerging from the so-called post-modern and globalised world. Economic globalisation has to a large extent driven the way people have lived and settled in many parts of the world. As a result, people of different cultures and faith perspectives are living in close proximity to each other. This reality is a sign of our time that poses certain challenges for ministers, such as how to deal with different perceptions around illness, death, suffering, joy, happiness, life after death, and so on. The meltdown of the global financial system will probably cause a fresh revisioning of how the markets should serve more adequately the peoples of the world. Such a rethinking will inevitably impact on how we perceive and think about each other culturally, politically and religiously. Will this cataclysmic economic meltdown bring us closer together or cause us to separate even further?

Theologically, seeing God's presence and action among us as the world, and Ireland particularly, grapples with this difficult economic event is a challenge for pastoral agents. Discovering how God is present and active interculturally will demand skilful dialogue within and among the different cultures and faith perspectives in Ireland and beyond. Conversation will be difficult because of difficulties around language and the various cultural and religious perspectives in relation to issues like gender, societal roles, sexuality, and practices around life and death, among others. For Christians, the Christian tradition shows us how to carry out this conversation, and insights for ministry can be gleaned. For example, the historical Jesus, in the context of his time, always engaged people in dialogue. Jesus' conversation with the Samaritan woman at the well, his conversations with the Pharisees, his encounter with the Syrophoenician woman, his dealings with those on the margins, all demonstrate that God's presence and action is discovered through the actual process of conversation.

The economic crisis is a particular sign of our time that offers both opportunities and challenges for ministers and theologians. One opportunity for ministers is to be of a consoling, compassionate, understanding and empathetic presence. This means that ministers take time to listen deeply in order to physically understand the other; to listen empathically to the pains, the fears and the struggles for coherence in the midst of personal chaos. To be an effective minister in these economically challenging times is to learn how to have effective and intentional conversations about the priorities and values we hold to be very important for us and why. For example, do we value a caring society more than economic prosperity? How do we care for the aged, the young, the marginalised, the migrant, and others in need of care? For Christians, whatever the burning issues, at the heart of the conversation will be the story and vision of the Christian tradition.

In various ways, the following chapters are a starting point for beginning that conversation. This book is a conversation that brings together both the practice and the theory of theology and ministry. Our lived experience and our religious traditions are essential parts of that conversation to discover and uncover God's presence and action in our lived reality today.

These chapters hope to stimulate this conversation around particular issues related to pastoral theology and ministry in today's Church. Hopefully, the specific focus around conversation, identity, presence, structures and supervision will help in understanding the global and local context in which pastoral theology is practiced.

The challenge, and the opportunity, is to create zones of compassion within our communities of faith for people to feel cared for, recognised, valued and loved. These zones are found within the ministers' own lived experiences and within the lived experience of a faith community. Such zones of comfort and meaningful belonging can gather the suffering, the marginalised and the excluded into life-giving relationships with themselves, others and God. Zones of compassion can be reflected in the home, school and parish.

In the contemporary world, it is not strange to any of us that if something happens in another part of the world, it has implications for all of us, not just on an economic level, but also socially, religiously and politically. An obvious example of this global interdependence is the way that issues affecting oil markets in another part of the world affects prices and supply in Ireland. Another example is the way in which we are all affected financially by the global credit crunch, which has influenced how we live, work and spend our money. We are now learning that what happens in America, Australia, Africa, or the Middle East has direct and indirect implications for the lives of everyone. We are learning about global warming and how the melting of the ice caps in Antarctica affects us in our part of the world. Theology is also affected by this global interdependence.

Theology – the science of God's revelation and presence – is very much impacted by what happens in the historical, social, political, religious and economic contexts anywhere on the planet. Though theology is done contextually, it is an interdependent reality as contexts are related to each other because of the constants of faith, truth, love, justice, compassion, forgiveness, suffering and life and death that exist in every context. For example, when the tsunami hit Indonesia at Christmastime 2004, many around the world wondered how God was present and active or absent and passive in this particular catastrophe. People wondered what the meaning of suffering was in that particular local context as well as reflecting upon the meaning of suffering in their own lived contexts. People turned to their own cultural and religious traditions for answers. Readers may think of other examples of contexts in which we reflect theologically and see how God's presence, or absence, for that matter, is revealed and experienced.

Readers can begin with any of the chapters in their study of ministry and their discovery of who Jesus is for them. The first contribution by Timothy Radcliffe focuses on the need for conversation in the Church today. He posits that '... all pastoral care is fundamentally conversation, a tiny hint of the conversation which is God. And conversation begins with recognition'. What is so fresh about Radcliffe is his understanding of young people, especially the new 'generation Y', that is, those in the 15–25 age group. An acknowledgement and understanding of this group is vital for the life of the Church into the future. Jesus recognised the young people and noted how the Kingdom of God belonged to them. In his ministry Jesus knew the significance of recognising people, like the lepers, the tax collectors and the marginalised. Recognition of people is at the heart of effective conversation and, according to Radcliffe, that conversation needs to highlight the importance of three aspirations for people in the so-called global village: happiness, freedom and beauty.

In the second chapter, a detailed overview of the intercultural reality of pastoral presence in the contemporary world is presented. Influenced by my experiences with Clinical Pastoral Education (CPE) and bereavement, I offer insights into how we can be more effective in our presence to those who may be marginalised, living through fractured relationships, suffering, imprisoned, or close to dying. Personal stories are also included as to my own path to effective ministry, and, like Radcliffe, I suggest that conversation is at the core of ministry. As mentioned earlier, the multicultural and multi-religious reality of Ireland today impacts on ministry in the way we are challenged by language and the struggle to interpret what others are really saying to us. Ministers are challenged by the different cultural and religious understandings around suffering, dignity, gender, role and societal expectations. This chapter explores some aspects of an effective intercultural pastoral presence. As well as situating pastoral presence in the broader world context and the Christian theological experience of incarnation, an outline of how one might conduct a meaningful and life-giving conversation is explored. A list of some guiding principles for conducting a pastoral conversation is also offered.

Living Systems are analysed and explored by Anne Codd in the third chapter. Readers obtain a glimpse of the way in which each of us is enmeshed in a network of structures that organise our lives. Codd examines the impact organic structures or systems have on the way the Church community lives its vision in various contexts. The link between systems theory and theology reveals a unique opportunity for understanding how our ministry is both assisted and sometimes impeded by the structures that surround the construction of life-giving theology and meaningful ministry. Codd offers pointers and suggestions as to how we might manage and work effectively with the structure of the Church we have at present. Awareness of how systems work can be a great asset to ministers in order to forge an understanding of why people might feel the way they feel about the Church today.

The fourth chapter addresses the issue of quality in ministry and the role of supervision in creating life-giving spaces for support and nurture so that ministry can be effective and meaningful. Practitioner Michael Carroll outlines in great detail the significance of supervision in the everyday life of the minister. Supervision in ministry is a growing profession in Ireland and beyond. More and more, ministers and others from the various caring professions recognise that if people are to be well cared for, the carers need to take care of themselves. Carroll points out that sport professionals, artists, musicians and others take great care of the gifts and talents they have by taking care of themselves. Likewise, ministers need to understand what it is they need to take care of so that they are effectual and helpful in ministry.

Finally, the last chapter looks towards the future, and Bairbre de Búrca offers some helpful ideas and suggestions on how to move on from the present position. In five essential steps, de Búrca continues the conversations by 'attempting to weave together the rich threads gathered from the papers within a framework of dialogue with self, dialogue within families, dialogue within communities, dialogue with the threat to the Cosmos and dialogue with the Judeo-Christian tradition'. A more detailed list and explanation of the signs of the times are provided in the chapter, which will help the reader come to terms with some of the challenges and opportunities in ministry.

At the end of each chapter are reflective questions. They are provided to help centre the reader's own thinking about theology and ministry. These open-ended questions, in a limited way, help the reader to claim and name their own life-giving theology. These questions arose from the reflective group process that was at the core of the pastoral conference, with open-ended focusing questions being offered to small groups. Participants at the conference had an important opportunity to engage with the ideas and suggestions put to them by the speakers, and now readers will get a taste of this reflective process as they engage with these reflective questions.

NOTE

1. See Terry A. Veling, *Practical Theology: 'On Earth as It Is in Heaven'*, New York, Maryknoll: Orbis Books, 2005, p. 17.

CHAPTER ONE

PASTORAL CARE IN THE GLOBAL VILLAGE

Timothy Radcliffe

When I prepared this chapter I had quite a time imagining whom I would be addressing. I read the brochure for the conference several times, trying to intuit the expectations. I discovered that 'this conference will focus on uncovering the intercultural face of God emerging from the post-modern and globalised world'. That sounded very impressive and I imagined people struggling with the post-modern angst of philosophers like Derrida and Foucault. And then I read that 'it is envisaged that this conference will be of interest to many people engaged in pastoral theological reflection within families, community centres, parishes, schools, hospitals, nursing homes, prisons, and other workplaces'. And I then thought that such people do not have the time or energy to labour through French philosophers when they come back home at night.

THE SIGNIFICANCE OF CONVERSATION

I start in this way to make a more fundamental point, which is that all pastoral care should spring out of conversation. I would have liked to have been with you for a while, shared a few pints and discovered what was tugging at your hearts before speaking. In the beginning was the Word. God alone has the first word, and we join in the conversation which the Word has initiated. All pastoral care, all preaching, even in the global village, is essentially dialogical. This is not because when you visit people in hospital or prison you must lull them into a false sense of security by first talking about Manchester United or the weather and then, when their defences are down, suddenly bring in Jesus. Christianity is a faith founded on conversation. We believe in the man who ambled around the Holy Land two thousand years ago, talking with those he met: the woman at the well, the blind man at the pool, beggars and lepers, tax collectors and prostitutes. The Word was made flesh in Jesus' conversations.

The word 'homily' comes from a Greek word which originally meant 'to converse'. Homilies should not be party political broadcasts launched from the invulnerability of the pulpit. They are moments in the conversation of God's people. They should help us to talk to each other. The Church is sustained by our innumerable conversations. St Catherine of Siena said that there is no greater pleasure than to talk about God with one's friends. And the preacher must always remember the old adage: you have two ears and one mouth and should use them accordingly.

If Jesus was a man of conversation, it is because the Trinity is the eternal, loving, equal, undominative conversation of God. Herbert McCabe OP wrote that sharing the life of the Trinity is like a young child listening to a fantastic conversation of adults in a pub:

> Think for a moment of a group of three or four intelligent adults relaxing together in one of those conversations that have really taken off. They are being witty and responding quickly to each other – what in Ireland they call 'the Crack'.[1] Serious ideas may be at issue, but no one is being serious. Nobody is being pompous or solemn (nobody is preaching). There are flights of fancy. There are jokes and puns and irony and mimicry and disrespect and self-parody ... Now this child is like us when we hear about the Trinity.[2]

The idea of dialogue is held in suspicion by some people in the Church. It is seen to smack of relativism, of suggesting that all theological positions and faiths are equal, of giving up on truth. But I would suggest that since what is at the heart of the gospel is Jesus, the man who conversed with us, and ultimately, the conversation that is the Trinity, then we can *only* talk truthfully of our faith in dialogue. To do otherwise would be like a pacifist beating up his opponents for disagreeing with him. I was at the Lambeth Conference in 2008 [meeting of the archbishops and bishops of the Anglican Church], and for the Anglican Church, one of the hot topics is: 'Do we dialogue with Islam, or seek to convert Muslims?' We can only share our faith with Muslims if we dialogue. And all conversation leads to conversion, with both partners being called to conversion. What form that conversion takes is in God's hands.

One of my brethren, Pierre Claverie, was the bishop of Oran, Algeria, until he was assassinated in 1996. His passion was dialogue with Islam. He, literally, gave his life to it. His story is documented in a beautiful book entitled *A Life Poured Out* by Jean Jacques Pérennès OP. Pierre's conversation with Islam led to conversion. There was his conversion, as he discovered Christ in the face of his Muslim friends. There was the conversion of his Muslim friends, who became better Muslims. And some of them, at the risk to their lives, became Christians.

JESUS' MISSION BEGINS WITH RECOGNITION

How do we begin a conversation? Jesus' mission always starts with recognition. He recognises Nathaniel as the person he has seen under the fig tree; he recognises little Zacchaeus up the tree; he recognises Mary in the garden. And because he recognises them, then they may recognise him in return. This is more than saying, 'Dear Nathaniel, we met last week at the fish market'. Jesus recognises people because, in a sense, he knows them from within. He is the Word of God, the one through whom all things came to be. He recognises strangers because he is the Son of God the creator who gives them being. And does it sound utterly silly to suggest that if we share the life of God lived by his Spirit, then we too somehow, dimly, recognise people from within? Saints like Padre Pio are often said to know you and what you have done before you have said a word, which is why someone like Graham Green was very nervous meeting him, as indeed I would have been too! If we are close to God, the giver of all existence, then we are in touch with the being of the other, even if very obscurely. That is the basis of all pastoral experience.

Many people in the Church are wounded by our failure to grant that recognition. Women most obviously, in our patriarchal Church, but often the poor, or ethnic minorities, or gay people, may feel invisible, or only seen from outside. In Lima I heard of a photographic exhibition of street kids, where under the photo of one desolate waif was written: '*Saben que existo, pero no me ven*': 'They know that I exist, but they do not see me.' They know that I exist as a statistic, as a menace, as a problem, but they do not see me. William James wrote:

> No more fiendish punishment could be devised, if such a thing were physically possible, than that one should be turned loose in society and remain absolutely unnoticed by all the members thereof. If no one turned around when we entered, answered when we spoke, or minded what we did, but if every person we met 'cut us dead', and acted as if we were non-existent things, a kind of rage and impotent despair would before long well up in us, from which the cruellest bodily torture would be a relief.[3]

Pope Benedict XVI wrote in *Deus caritas est*: 'Seeing with the eyes of Christ, I can give to others much more than their outward necessities; I can give them the look of love for which they crave.'[4] We live in a society in which increasing numbers of people are invisible. Our names are recorded in a thousand ways, our emails are monitored, CCTV cameras record our movements. Big Brother is always watching, but we may feel unseen. These eyes, like the lens of a camera, merely record the surfaces.

That is why 'respect' is such a big word on urban streets these days. Urban violence is often the desperate search for 'respect', for recognition. Erinma Bell, the founder of a peace group in Manchester called Carisma and recent recipient of an MBE, said of gang members: 'They've nothing else in their lives apart from their desperate need to feel a sense of power over others on the street ... Their days and nights revolve around whether they feel "disrespected" by their peers or whether some petty grievance or other has flared up into a score that needs to be settled.'[5]

Maybe that is why icons play such a big role in many people's spirituality today. We do not so much look at icons as let them look at us. According to Rowan Williams, 'the skill of looking at icons, the discipline of "reading" them, is indeed the strange skill of letting yourself be seen, be read'.[6] In a world in which we often feel invisible, or just seen from outside, as objects, we need to bask in the gaze of Christ or Our Lady or a saint who looks at us benevolently, who gives us, in Pope Benedict's words, the look of love for which we crave. It offers us the compassionate gaze which the CCTV camera does not give.

So, all pastoral care is fundamentally conversation, a tiny hint of the conversation which is God. And conversation begins with recognition. What are the particular challenges of recognition in the global village?

The brochure for this pastoral conference quotes Dietrich Bonhoeffer: 'Am I really what others say of me? Or am I only what I know of myself?' I would suggest that it is precisely in conversation that I inch towards a proper sense of self-identity. And this happens because my sense of who I am is in negotiation with other people's understanding of my identity. I do have some privileged sense of who I am. I know lots of things about myself that no one else knows, thanks be to God. But it is also true that I discover who I am in other people's eyes. Gentle conversation helps me towards a sense of identity that is a convergence between who I know myself to be and who I discover myself to be with the other. Friendship allows us both to discover who we are with each other. So a conversation is pastoral if through it the identities of both people are open to evolution and discovery. I will discover a little bit more of who I am with you, and vice versa. Rowan Williams' latest book on Dostoevsky demonstrates that this is the key to his understanding of the novel, the open-ended discovery of identity in dialogue.

But this respectful, exploratory conversation starts with who people think they are, with the face they present to the world. That face may be in part a mask, even a disguise, but it is where one begins. If I meet someone who claims to be punk or a goth, or indeed delights in being rich or whatever, then that is where we begin. When Jesus talked with the rich man, he first loved him as he was, rolling in his wealth, before, at a second stage, Jesus could invite him to be poor. He feasted and drank with the prostitutes and tax collectors as they were. The invitation to discover a deeper identity could come later.

Here we get to a major challenge for the Church, and I confess that I do not know the answer to it. Many young people root their identities in families that are broken and 'irregular'. Their parents may be single, or living with serial partners, with children by different people or in a gay relationship. To recognise these young people is to recognise the relationships that they have. They will say to us, 'To accept me, you must accept those who are mine'. If we seem to trash their families, in the name of the Christian vision of the family life, then they will think that we are trashing them. I do cherish the Christian vision of family – a man and a woman living together for life and open to the gift of children. We must champion the family. The consequences of its fragility are wounding for society and especially for children. But I must begin where people are, with their fidelities that define their lives. We must hang out with them, accept their hospitality and be their guests. There is no other beginning. So the first stage of pastoral care is conversation, and conversation is based on recognition, and recognition includes beginning where people are, with the identities they claim. Of course my own identity will be called into question as well!

The next question is: what shall we share in our conversation? What will make a conversation come alive? I think that we need to find concerns, topics, aspirations which we both share and yet which we perceive differently. If what tugs at our hearts is utterly different, then conversation may be hard. And if we have exactly the same views, then it will be boring! I would suggest three areas where Christianity intersects with the aspirations of people in the global village: happiness, freedom and beauty. I had thought of talking about truth, a topic dear to Dominicans, but there is not time for everything.

HAPPINESS

People seek happiness. This is the universal human aspiration. Augustine wrote: 'Everyone wants to be happy. There is no one who will not agree with me on this almost before the words are out of my mouth.'[7] Christianity, certainly in the tradition of Augustine and Thomas Aquinas, believes that we are made to find our happiness in God. So, fundamental to our pastoral interaction is the question of happiness.

The happiness that young people seek is in fact threatened and fragile. Happiness is hard to attain in a fragmented and competitive society. It is menaced by broken families, drug abuse, urban violence and imprisonment. Perhaps even more fundamentally, happiness is often today experienced as an obligation. One must be happy, otherwise one is a failure. And so there is much shame attached to feeling sad. It must be disguised. A survey of Generation Y concludes: 'Sadness is not easily acknowledged in the face of "achievable" happiness. For this reason, sadness may be a powerful source of hidden shame and loneliness for young people.'[8] One reason for the epidemic of suicides among the young is an imperative to be joyful which they cannot sustain.

One explanation for this shame for our sorrow is that we have often psychologised it and called it depression. We have turned sorrow, the ordinary human response to life's suffering, into a mental illness that is to be treated. Two American authors, Horwitz and Wakefield, wrote a book called *The Loss of Sadness: How Psychiatry Transformed Normal Sorrow into Depressive Disorder*. Of course depression is a real illness which we must treat, but millions of people, they assert, are not suffering from it; they are just sad. And that is the healthy reaction to some situations, and one must learn to live it fruitfully, creatively, with the help of one's friends and one's faith.

So in our pastoral conversation I hope that we can embody Christian happiness. And this is odd because it is large enough to have a space for sadness, the sadness that is the inevitable consequence of being alive in a world in which there is suffering. At the end of Matthew's gospel, Jesus tells the disciples to go and make disciples of all nations, 'teaching them to observe all that I have commanded you' (Mt 28:20). And scholars are largely in agreement that what are in question are the Beatitudes. The disciples are sent to teach the beatitudes, which embody God's bittersweet happiness: happy are the poor, for theirs in the kingdom of heaven; happy are those who mourn, for they shall be comforted; happy are those who are persecuted for righteousness' sake, for theirs is the kingdom of heaven. This is a strange happiness that is big enough for every sorrow, and that is because it is not the happiness of any single moment but of the whole of Jesus' life, which goes from birth to death and resurrection. The sorrow of Good Friday is held in a story which is pointed to the joy of the Father.

So this is a happiness which we must embody if our words are to have authority. It is said that St Francis' preaching made even the fish happy. As a Dominican, I wonder how you can tell a happy fish from a sad one. The most joyful saints are also the most sorrowful, like Francis, or Dominic, who laughed by day with his brethren and wept at night with God. The Abbot Primate of the Benedictines, Notker Wolf, invited some Japanese Buddhist and Shintuist monks to come and stay for two weeks in the monastery of St Ottilien, Bavaria. When they were asked what struck them, they replied, 'The joy. Why are Catholic monks such joyful people?' And it is not only monks who should be infected by this joy. It is a tiny glimpse of the beatitude for which we are all created. It is the exuberance of those who have drunk the new wine of the gospel. The new wine which makes you drunk was the favourite metaphor of the early Dominicans for the gospel.

FREEDOM

And there is freedom. The European Values Surveys have consistently shown that one of the most fundamental values of young people is freedom. Often this is the freedom of the consumer, to buy what he or she wants. The young generally value money not because they are materialistic, for they are not. Rather, it gives them the freedom to go where they want and be whom they wish.

An advertisement for Levi's jeans briefly became a potent symbol of this freedom from constraint. It showed people running on walls, along felled trees, jumping over chasms.[9] In France there is Yamakasi, from a Congolese root meaning 'strong person, strong spirit, strong body'. It is a sport whereby one runs through the city turning barriers into steps toward freedom, walls into jumping places. One dances through, over and around all that tries to hem one in. In fact young people are ever less free, more controlled, watched by more CCTV cameras, recorded and even imprisoned. Hence the attractive freedom of the Internet where you can abolish distance, recreate yourself, be anyone you wish. You can join a chat room with people on the other side of the world, and disconnect when you have had enough. If you get bored with a TV programme you can zap to another channel. This you cannot do with a boring sermon!

If the Church is to proclaim the gospel, then we need to meet this hunger for freedom, accept it and lead people on to the deeper freedom of Christ. This is hard because the Church is usually understood as opposing personal autonomy, telling people what they are not allowed to do. As we have seen, religion is feared to mean 'Thou shalt not ...' The Church does not come across as an oasis of wild freedom, the intoxicating freedom of Jesus, and until it does, then our words will not mean much. Ultimately we need to incarnate the dizzy freedom of Jesus who gave away his life.

BEAUTY

Finally, let me say just a few words about beauty. In St John's gospel, Jesus says: 'When I am lifted up, I will draw all to myself' (Jn 12:42). Jesus does not bully people into the Church, nor offer belief as a lifestyle option, or the ultimate insurance policy. He draws people to himself. He attracts us by the beauty of his life and his teaching. Gerry O'Collins SJ says in *Jesus: A Portrait*:

> We gladly give our hearts to what is beautiful. We fall in love with beautiful men and women. Those people who are beautiful possess an instant appeal. We hope that they are also

good and truthful, but it is their beauty that catches and holds our attention. Jesus is the beauty of God in person. When we fall in love with his beauty, we are well on the way to accepting his truth and imitating his goodness.[10]

When I was a boy at Downside, I think that my faith was kept alive by the utter beauty of the great Abbey church and of the singing of the monks. In our society the teaching of the Church is often experienced as arrogant, as intolerant of other beliefs, as oppressive. I do not believe that it is, but that is the subject of another chapter. But where there is resistance to teaching, people can be seduced by beauty. Ann Lamott tells of a woman who simply refused to have anything to do with a man dying of AIDS, until she was touched by the beauty of music: 'Maybe it is because music is as physical as it gets; your essential rhythm is your heartbeat; your essential sound the breath. We're walking temples of noise, and when you add tender hearts to this mix, it somehow lets us meet in places we couldn't get to any other way.'[11]

Beauty is one of the ways in which our faith may be in dynamic contact with modernity. We should treasure it wherever we find it, whether the artists are believers or not. And we should offer a beautiful liturgy and art as ways of sharing our faith that do not bully or moralise, but gently offer a new way of seeing the world.

I think that we need a new aesthetic to share our faith with our world. Every renaissance of the Church has gone with a fresh beauty. The renewal of the Church in the twelfth and thirteenth centuries went with the renewal of Gregorian chant. The Reformation and Counter-Reformation each had their music; the Methodist revival was linked with the massive creation of hymns. We need artists – singers, musicians, painters, poets, novelists, film directors – to incarnate a glimpse of God's beauty. And we need to be in touch with the creative people of our society and receive their gifts.

Conclusion

Pastoral care in the global village is founded on conversation. Genuine conversation converts both partners. If we reach out in conversation, it will change us as well. When Jesus conversed with the Canaanite woman, he at first resisted her demands because she was a pagan and he was sent to the lost sheep of the house of Israel. But she led him beyond where he had been. No conversation is real if it does not change us too.

It begins with recognition. We know the other person from within, since if we share the life of God the creator, then we have a tiny participation in God's knowledge of the other. And if we recognise them, then they may recognise us too. In any conversation the identity of both partners is both given and discovered. I do know myself in some ways, but I also discover myself in the eyes of the other. We must therefore begin with a deep respect for the identities that our interlocutors claim. If that is where they are, then we must be there too, even if we may hope to eventually discover together a deeper identity, as God's own children.

Our conversation must be founded upon what touches us, our deepest desires. And I have suggested that three of these are happiness, freedom and beauty. There are others. Our words will have authority if they are embedded in a joy which is large enough for sorrow, a freedom deep enough to encompass utter generosity, and a hint of the beauty with which Jesus will draw all to himself.

Questions for Reflection

I.   How can we offer the young Christ's look of recognition?
II. What inhibits our Christian joy?
III. How can we enter more fully into Christ's freedom?

NOTES

1. Far be it for me to correct Herbert McCabe's Irish, but I am told it should be 'craic'!

2. Herbert McCabe, *God, Christ and Us*, London: Continuum, 2003, p. 115.

3. From *The Principles of Psychology*, Boston, 1890, quoted by Alain de Botton in *Status Anxiety*, London: Vintage, 2004, p. 15.

4. Pope Benedict XVI, *Deus caritas est*, 18.

5. Amelia Hill, *The Observer*, 12 August 2007.

6. *Lost Icons*, p. 185.

7. *De moribus ecclesiae catholicase*, 3.4 SCE 18.

8. Sara Savage and Sylvia Collins-Mayo, *Making Sense of Generation Y: The World View of 15–25 year-olds*, London: Church House, 2006, p. 48.

9. Ibid., p. 40.

10. London: Darton, Longman & Todd, 2008, p. 1.

11. Ibid., p. 65.

CHAPTER TWO

THE INTERCULTURAL REALITY OF PASTORAL PRESENCE

Thomas G. Grenham

MAY YOU AWAKEN TO THE MYSTERY OF BEING HERE
AND ENTER THE QUIET IMMENSITY OF YOUR OWN PRESENCE.
John O'Donohue[1]

Has anyone recently asked you: Who are you? Who are you as a chaplain, minister, pastor, carer, theologian or other professional? Or, who do people around you say that you are? What do you tell them? Do you ask your friends or colleagues what people are saying about you? Jesus' question to his disciples: 'Who do you say that I am?' is very significant for ministry. This question is rooted in a deep understanding of the meaning of an effective pastoral presence and how the person's identity is shaped, recognised and confirmed by the responses received. This was a significant question that Jesus posed. Culture, religion and society play a crucial role in the reply to the question. The answer to the question is further enriched or challenged by interaction with the diversity of cultures and the plurality of religions.

Ireland is no longer the predominantly mono-cultural and mono-religious entity it was some twenty years ago. It is changing fast and shifting from a predominantly Catholic country to embrace a variety of religious and secular perspectives. Are we any better off, especially in the way we pastorally care for our people on both a national and personal level? How present are we to one another in the Ireland of today and, from a national point of view, how present are we internationally to one another, especially to our brothers and sisters most in need? Two things will be explored here – pastoral presence and how it is affected by a changing cultural context. Defining what is meant by 'pastoral presence' can be challenging. I perceive it more like an 'awakening' to self and to the relationship with the other.

'AWAKENING' TO PRESENCE

Of all the experiences I have critically reflected upon and continue to reflect upon around pastoral presence, I offer, from my own ministry, two cutting-edge examples of when this concept actually became enlightened deep within my own consciousness as a pastoral agent. This is not to say that I was not ministerially present or available to people during all my other ministries over the years. Rather, these so-called 'aha' or 'awakening' chosen moments of presence highlighted a deepening awareness for me that increased my level of understanding of how to be an empathic pastoral presence within all pastoral contexts.

The first experience concerns a Clinical Pastoral Education (CPE) supervisor who once asked a small group of participants what was the most important element of a pastoral visit? Many insights surfaced, including empathy, listening, bedside manner, compassion and so on. One of the participants said that a meaningful presence was necessary in any pastoral visit. The supervisor seemed pleased with this assertion. This led to a discussion on what constitutes or defines a meaningful and helpful pastoral presence. As one of the participants in that group, I became very interested as to why this should be so important. I had imagined that the meaning of a pastoral presence would be something fairly obvious. After all, I assumed that when I entered a parish hall, a hospital ward, or a classroom, I would be noticed, recognised and valued because of my physical existence and demeanour if nothing else. Surely this would be enough to create a space or an atmosphere for a meaningful pastoral encounter with the other person/patient. Would my physical presence not be sufficient to provide a safe space to interact with me in the pastoral visit and provide the space for the other to engage with me? Needless to say, I discovered I had much to learn in understanding the meaning of pastoral presence.

My other example is related to two significant family bereavements in 2007. My younger sister and father died within three months of each other. Whatever I learned in my CPE studies ten years earlier about the power of presence, these events around bereavement would further deepen my understanding of authentic relational presence. It helped me to be more available to others in deep pain and distress. I learned that the power of presence in these difficult situations drives home the significance of life-giving relationship and meaningful belonging in our life-world. These particular events required a presence that was painful, that was helpless, that was available and that was cherished. The experience of presence among the dying in one's own family solidified for me how valuable and significant we are as caregivers or ministers. I learned about the appeal of genuine human empathy, the role of prayer, the importance of silence and the impact of some religious symbols such as water and light. This sense of walking in others' shoes struck home in a different way. I feel that the underlying issue in this kind of family presence was the capacity to journey with someone who is dying and to attend to the dying person's questions, worries, fears and doubts. For example, questions like what happens to me when I die? Where will I go? Will I go to heaven? Was there a purpose to my life? Will I be remembered when I am gone? and so on, are part of this questioning. I can't tell if there is a particular skill in staying with these questions, only that it feels sometimes that one stumbles along in being actually present and eventually something very worthwhile and life-giving emerges in the relationship.

A key part is recognising that we don't have the perfect answers to these questions. The challenge for pastoral agents/ministers is to live and be attentive to the questions that are articulated and not run away or avoid them. Perhaps the other important piece is the inevitable reality of being disturbed in the exercise of ministry – the disturbing or triggering of one's own fears, doubts and concerns around suffering, imprisonment, poverty, punishment, discrimination, illness, relationship breakdown, death and dying, and so on. We might ask what our own questions around these events are? What is it that gets disturbed in us when we meet vulnerability and fragility in others? For example, what is triggered in us when we engage with a family member or close acquaintance who is dying. Do we disengage in any way? Can we hold the sacred dying space with them and just simply be present to their agony, to their anguish, to their terrible fear, to their loneliness, and to their dying dreams? This kind of presence is not easy for anyone. There is no distinct and definitive arrival point when one can say I have arrived at being always fully present and attentive. Effective pastoral presence is characterised by a capacity to translate our own theology and spirituality through the lens of our own losses, as a bridge to enter the space of others' disappointments, betrayals and hurts, in order to authentically enter their space and help them make sense of their suffering. Consequently, our own brokenness, struggles and vulnerabilities, if integrated, become our greatest resources for the embodiment of an effective pastoral presence. The key word here is *integration,* which is something to be worked at and learned over time.

Empowering pastoral presence is a journey, a pilgrim journey in becoming more mindful. It is a life-long journey of discovery about the self, others, God and the created world. In addition, pastoral presence is not something unique and pertinent to any one culture or religious context. Rather, presence or presences implies a self-emptying – letting go of one's own biases, judgements, status, privilege and sense of position, so as to be free to 'crossover' to the other person's cultural and religious experience. An effective and quality presence in a very fragmented world can be the glue to foster caring relational communities everywhere. A universal observation to make is that all cultures seem to experience a sense of woundedness, loss and fragmentation. The skilful pastoral agent is open to learning and understanding the ways in which people feel pain, loss and suffering within the specific cultural and religious reality of their lived experience. A respectful dialogue or conversation, with silence at times, is helpful in providing space for a meaningful, quality pastoral presence in such circumstances. Given what I have already said about my own experiences around presence, I would like to ask the foundational question again: What is a pastoral presence?

DEFINITION OF PRESENCE

Philosopher John O'Donohue writes:

> When we speak of an individual, we speak of his presence. Presence is the way a person's individuality comes toward you. Presence is the soul texture of the person. When we speak of this presence in relation to a group of people, we refer to it as atmosphere or ethos. The ethos of a workplace is a very subtle group presence.[2]

Presence is about an ability to 'be with' another person or an ability to enter the space of another person. Presence is about 'being' rather than 'doing'. It is about mindfulness – actively attentive to self, other, God and the created world. Presence is about relationship with self and other. Other represents another person, a transcendent reality such as God, or the created environment around us. Presence is about an inner capacity of 'being with' and resisting the urge to always 'fix'. The pastoral agent who is a non-anxious presence is attentive to the spiritual realities not always explicit. John Patton observes that:

> The pastoral carer, whether laity or clergy, is present to the person cared for in a particular kind of relationship – one that 're-presents' the presence of God through relationship to the person cared for. Pastoral carers 're-present' or remind persons of God by remembering and hearing, and affirm by their action that God continues to hear and remember them.[3]

To be present to oneself is to be in relationship with one's own feelings, intellect, emotions and physicality. An appropriate presence with the other assumes presence to oneself in order to adequately and genuinely empathise with the suffering other. This is to say that the minister understands their own needs around care, recognition and vulnerability but does not burden the other with these needs. These needs are appropriately bracketed or parked and addressed in a different space such as pastoral supervision.

Presence also entails a healthy awareness of one's own mortality. Our death is a constant companion. John O'Donohue was very much aware of this in his own lifetime. He states that:

> There is a presence who walks the road of life with you. This presence accompanies your every moment. It shadows your every thought and feeling. On your own, or with others, it is always there with you. When you were born, it came out of the womb with you, but with the excitement at your arrival, nobody noticed it. Though this presence surrounds you, you may still be blind to its companionship. The name of this presence is death.[4]

A healthy awareness of our own process of dying and death is important. I believe that an integrated sense of one's personal dying will greatly enhance the quality of presence for someone in the actual process of journeying out of this life. This won't be easy to achieve and will demand digging deep our personal wells as we journey into the depths of our being in the world. However, in a relationship, even when I am absent from the dying person because I am absent from my own suffering and dying, I am still present because of the relationship that I have already established with the one dying or suffering. I feel that we can be consoled by this reality as pastoral carers and ministers, because we are not perfect. We are also wounded and vulnerable in our roles as pastoral agents. However, where there is a meaningful relationship there is a 'presence' even in 'absence'.

How do we know as pastoral caregivers and ministers that we are present to another person? Could it be that we are actually more absent than present in some or all of our pastoral visitations to those who are ill, marginalised, dying, and so on? What are the blocks, barriers or distractions that prevent an effective life-giving presence? How can we be helped to cross these road blocks to an effective mindfulness in ourselves? To help throw some light on these questions, I will outline a personal experience.

I remember my first visit to a patient, who was recovering from a tracheostomy procedure after being diagnosed with cancer in a Boston hospital. The person had a tube placed in his trachea so he could breathe. I had never seen this before, and I was at a loss when I discovered that the patient could not speak. This upset my prepared pastoral plan as I had assumed that patients could always speak! Now how was I going to embody an empathic pastoral presence for this man who seemed very welcoming? My first reaction as a young priest was to run away as quickly as I could, maintaining some sense of dignity, I thought. Was this an experience of absence on my part? Or was it an experience of vulnerability, inadequacy and anxiousness? Perhaps the patient could relate to my discomfort as in some ways we were kindred spirits in that moment. The patient could not speak and neither was I able to speak. However, the scene would leave an indelible mark upon me as a minister. When I told the story to my supervisor, I was invited to return to the man again, accompanied by the supervisor, who in a very non-anxious manner modelled for me how to be a healing presence in this pastoral encounter.

I was greatly impressed by the 'ways of being' I evidenced in the supervisor. The supervisor did not reflect a distracted presence, but was gentle, calm, accepting, unhurried, introduced herself and then me to the patient, seemed at ease, and noted the photo of his family on the top of the bedside locker. This detail had eluded me completely. I was relieved at being introduced to the patient. My anxiety was lowered and subsequently, after much reflection and analysis, I was able to befriend my fear of the 'unknown' and visit other patients and be an authentic healing presence for them.

Through this experience, my own fear of the unfamiliar such as the sight of tubes, serious illness, speechlessness, disability and my fear of death became defused, which heretofore had hindered my ability to be fully available and present to others facing death, serious illness or loss. I realised that my humanity and vulnerabilities, if integrated and embraced, become crucial links to helping me enter the space of another person in their suffering. Such appropriate integration becomes the essence of quality presence, even though it does not always feel that integration has taken place. We cannot stop feeling and perceiving, and our comfort zones can be challenged by what we see, hear and know. Intuition is significant for meaningful presence.

INTUITION AND PRESENCE

Intuition entails a deeper level of interactive knowing between the minister and person, counselee, patient, client. Such knowing might be felt physically deep within the structure of the body. It is an instinctive knowing. It has been termed a 'gut feeling' and is a significant emotional component in realising an effective presence to the self, others and a transcendent reality. Being intuitive implies a capacity to recognise the significance of a quality presence in the pastoral relationship. It is the ability 'to see within' without explanations. O'Donohue notes that 'Presence is something you sense and know, but cannot grasp. It engages us but we can never capture its core; it remains somehow elusive'.[5] O'Donohue further notes that 'All the great art forms strive to create living icons of presence'.[6]

Intuition is a deep way of 'knowing' and is enhanced by our degree of self-awareness and self-knowledge. The ability to draw on intuition is an important ingredient for an intercultural and interreligious communication. Intuition is the ability to see below the surface of conversations and the non-verbal and this can be a great gift for developing quality in ministry.

QUALITY MINISTRY AND CHRISTIAN PRESENCE

At the core of a quality pastoral ministry is the notion of an effective relational presence. The presence becomes effective when the other can respond in ways that evoke a sense that they feel heard, understood and respected as persons of dignity in their broken condition. There is a sense that the sacred is evoked whether explicit or implicit in every visit, whether that is always clear or not. The patient, client, parishioner, prisoner or refugee may allude to God or to experiences in the Church community or simply to no particular religious experience. Ministers need to respect that and not proselytise in favour of religious perspectives that they find helpful.

Even though there may be no explicit mention of God, or the patient is an adherent of a different religion, Christian ministers, who hold to the vision and story of the Christian tradition, believe that the Spirit of God is manifested in every person, culture and religion. For Christians, their agency as pastoral caregivers, counsellors, supervisors, spiritual directors and so on, is a reflection of that presence of God. The pastoral encounter represents a symbolic presence of God or some other transcendent reality. The quality of their presence to the client can radiate God's healing power. Of course the opposite can be communicated as well, such that God is reflected as distant and non-caring. The distance or absence of God can be experienced by the demeanour, gesture, words and attitude of the minister. However, learning and embodying a sense of *effective presence* is a life-long journey of discovery, practice and insight. Some practitioners seem to have a natural gift of powerful presence while others have to work at recognising that they can be a source of powerful presence. Brazilian educator Paulo Freire observes that:

> Our being in the world is far more than just 'being'. It is a 'presence', a 'presence' that is relational to the world and to others. A 'presence' that, in recognising another presence as 'not I', recognises its own self. A 'presence' that can reflect upon itself, that knows itself as presence, that can intervene, can transform, can speak of what it does, but that can also take stock of, compare, evaluate, give value to, decide, break with, and dream.[7]

A meaningful quality presence begins with 'centring' or focusing on the visit. Establishing a relationship takes time and may not happen instantly. Gradually a relationship may emerge through showing respect and building trust. Trust is so important for a vulnerable person, and when it comes to dealing with difference and diversity, there needs to be an awareness of this reality without being hypersensitive, which can erode trust. Skills in empathetic listening, open-ended statements, appropriate comments and observations, eye contact, appropriate physical gestures, caring disposition, and so on, are part of this pastoral conversation for healing. Reflect back a key word or part of a sentence. Ask for clarification. Use silence well – give the person time. Conversation needs to take place so that the reflection upon the pastoral action is effective, especially for the client. This reflection draws upon the lived human experiences and the life-giving cultural and religious traditions of the client for greater insight and healing. The minister in this conversation is a conduit for love and compassionate care. Two important phrases for effecting pastoral ministry are: 'Dún do bhéal' (close your mouth) and 'Éist' (listen). If the minister is doing most of the talking, raise the red flag! It is helpful to recognise that 'words' can be distancing and that silence is not empty. Silence can create a connection of intimacy and closeness or presence. If there is absence instead of presence, what could we expect to happen? The terror of meaninglessness raises its head.

In the absence of presence:
The terror of meaninglessness

Theologians Patricia O'Connell Killen and John de Beer observe that:

> For human beings the drive for meaning is stronger than the drive for physical survival. We need to make sense of what happens to us, to clothe our existence within an interpretative pattern that reflects back to us lives of integrity, coherence and significance. If we cannot, the will to live withers.[8]

O'Connell Killen and de Beer highlight the need for meaning as the underpinning for our basic survival and that this meaning is uncovered through the interpretation of our experience in a particular context. To do this interpretation well, we need an appropriate, life-giving presence grounded in the wisdom of the responsible carer. Addressing the blocks to life-giving meaning is important to allow a sense of personal freedom and wisdom to filter into the deepest recesses of a person's spirit. These blocks are manifested in all kinds of ways such as negative personal experiences reflected through painful relationships, hurtful events and abusive situations. Such blocks can be fearful spaces.

The absence of a life-giving presence on the part of a pastoral agent gives rise to such experiences as spiritual terror, emotional isolation, relational separation or disconnection from the world of meaningful belonging as well as other experiences of alienation, exclusion and loneliness. A patient or client who experiences a pastoral agent who is not fully present to them or seems distracted may feel discounted, stigmatised, unimportant, shamed, or even bullied.

Extrapolating from the difficulties of a lack of life-giving presence at the individual level and moving toward the national or international levels, a parallel is drawn. We can begin to realise that the lack of an effective pastoral or caring presence for the group, the community, the state and the international community may help us understand why we have so much misunderstanding and conflict in our world. It seems that the absence of life-giving presence creates a space in which devastating conflicts and wars emerge. A meaningful and inclusive presence on the part of governments, multinational companies, markets, cultures, religions, and so on, throughout the world means that perhaps the tragedy of 11 September 2001 in the United States, and subsequent terror attacks around the world, could be avoided. The so-called war on terror highlights for everyone the urgent need for an effective meaningful and life-giving international and intercultural mutual, respectful presence. The concerns around climate change and other ecological issues all involve a holistic presence in which we see ourselves and our created world as in significant relationship to our communities. Most particularly, pastoral care in these circumstances challenges every carer to attend to the suffering humanity and the suffering environment around them.

We are called to attend – to pay attention to what is happening around us. We are not called as ministers to solve all problems for everyone. Rather, we are present and available to others in order to support, empathise and stand in solidarity with them in their own struggles and help them discover for themselves solutions and 'answers' to what may be happening to them in their lives. It is about promoting, advocating and fostering a life-giving and safe space to grow, to heal, to transform and to live and die with dignity. Creating a life-giving space for healing and transformation is, as Bob Whiteside observes, '... the task of those called to pastor, whether as youth ministers, pastoral workers, priests etc., to create and maintain such a space – a compassionate space where people can enter in, be held, restored and transformed as they face the numerous issues in their lives'.[9] For this compassionate space to be fostered, the pastoral carer needs a secure, genuine, authentic pastoral identity. This is vital.

SHAPING A PASTORAL IDENTITY

When Jesus asked that question of his disciples, 'Who do you say that I am?', he may have indicated that he needed some clue as to the meaning of his own presence among them and the reason for his ministry. Or Jesus may have been testing the disciples to see if they had a sense of his pastoral identity and a sense of their own purpose as pastoral agents. It was in the conversation with them that clarity around Jesus' identity emerged. Peter responded with the insight, 'You are the Messiah'. A sense of personal and pastoral identity seemed to undergird Jesus' question. The answers he received when he asked the question first time around could confuse Jesus' identity with other known prophets until Peter clarified precisely who Jesus was: a saviour or liberator for their world. John Patton suggests that:

> Identity has been defined as the very 'core' of a person toward which everything else is ordered. It is something that, if one knows it, provides the 'clue' to a person. Identity is the specific uniqueness of a person, what really counts about him, quite apart from both comparison and contrast to others.[10]

In relation to shaping a secure and integrated pastoral identity, I am reminded of when the opposite was the reality in my own formation and training as a pastoral minister. During my CPE formation, I had the experience of what is known in United States hospitals as a code 99 emergency. My beeper went off and immediately I went to the relevant ward to discover that the patient was being attended to in an urgent manner. He was surrounded by medical staff anxiously caring for him. No part of the body was visible. In that moment, I wondered what need there was for me? What I had to offer was of little use in this extreme emergency, or so I thought. And to further add to my doubts, the nurse on the ward called out in a loud voice for all non-essential personnel to leave the room – she was looking at me. As I left the ward, I was full of doubt about whether or not I was really needed. After all, the chaplain or minister has few 'tools' and skills to help people in these emergencies. What can a chaplain 'do'? Over time, I did learn how to be a significant non-anxious healing presence in such circumstances for the clinical staff, patients and families. I learned that my presence as a chaplain made a unique and essential contribution by being a source of support, comfort, advocacy and healing for the community involved in these extreme emergencies. My identity as a pastoral agent eventually became shaped by practice and support from fellow colleagues in CPE and staff at the hospital. Some skills of communication were helpful in such extreme emergencies.

The cultural, societal and religious environments we live in are significant components in shaping our identities as individual persons and communities. Identity is a relational, interpersonal process. Culture is everything that engages human beings in the living of their lives. The ideas we have about each other, our behaviour, the meaning we interpret from experience, our emotions, the material artefacts that we gather, the food we eat and the languages we speak all point to a cultural framework in which we live and have our essential being or existence. Such identity is further influenced by a plurality of cultures and religions that we encounter in our ministry in Ireland today.

Every person is situated in a particular historical, cultural context and is primarily shaped by its contours, conditioned by its inherent logic, and emotionally embedded in its assumptions. Within the ambit of culture(s) are religious/spiritual dimensions that provide significant influences in the overall dynamic of personal and communal formation. Pastoral ministry is about entering the trenches or the mineshaft that is the human condition and coming face to face with situations and differences of all kinds: culture, religion, gender, sexual orientation, race, class, ethnicity, and so on. There are even divisions within these groupings, as no person holds the same precise viewpoint within any of these ways of being in the world. This is why learning the art of being present and available to the reality of the agonies and ecstasies (joys or sufferings) is so significant especially for men and women called to ministry. Men and women will experience ministry differently depending on the particular formation around gender and the prescribed societal rules in relation to gender. Needless to say, gender can be a block for some ministers, as indeed it can be for those who are being cared for or being ministered to by a pastor.

It is possible for some individuals to be physically present and not engage the spiritual/cultural meaning system of another for a variety of reasons. Even within the same family system, difference will be evident as each member relates differently to each other and has a unique interpretation of who they are in relation to their parents, grandparents and siblings. There may be a common interest/vision or a historical family legacy that holds the unit together. However, each member will experience their need to belong differently and this will surface many times in various kinds of conversations between themselves and in encounters with other carers and ministers. One area in which a conversation may help is within the sphere of our religious certainties and cultural prejudices, some of which we inherit at a very early age.

DEALING WITH RELIGIOUS CERTAINTIES AND CULTURAL BIAS

Much healing can happen if the philosophy or the theology of presence is incorporated into a meaningful and appropriate pastoral relationship. However, sometimes our own religious certainties and cultural bias can block that inner freedom to allow God be God in our lives.

The sense that my faith perspective is unsurpassed may be an unconscious attitude. The perception that my own cultural world view is the most congenial, beneficial, life-giving and meaningful for my life and maybe for others could influence the way we engage those who are 'different'. If it works for me, you should believe it, embrace it, select it and belong to it! How many of us believe this unconsciously?

During his time, the Pharisees, Lawyers and Sadducees had their comfort zones challenged by Jesus' encounters with them. However, they chose not to change because of their own bias for power, privilege and status. They were afraid to let go of a life-restricting image of themselves because of a fear of loss to their culturally and religiously established sense of identity within the community. It seems to me that a pre-requisite for being an authentic pastoral agent, possessing an effective presence, is an ability to open oneself to learning and growing and the possibility for personal transformation that occurs when we enter the space of another. Henri Nouwen often spoke of our agency as 'wounded to the wounded'. Our patients, our parishioners, our marginalised, our unemployed, our refugees, our prisoners and others in need make manifest to us the loving presence of God and they become our most profound teachers in inviting us to a deeper understanding of ourselves and the meaning of our vocation to ministry. We can be changed and transformed by those who die, those who suffer grievously, those who feel disillusioned, those who have lost hope and those who struggle on the margins of society. Yet, through all their suffering, there is a resilience to transcend the current painful reality and inspire others, including the minister. Suffering humanity has so much to teach us about life and its abundance. A theology of life-giving presence is helpful to understand how God is present to us and is with us in this constant human struggle to live a life of fulfilment, freedom and wisdom. Such a theological vision is interpersonal, intercultural and interreligious.

AN INTERCULTURAL THEOLOGY OF PRESENCE

From a Christian theological and spiritual perspective, life-giving presence is a presence that reflects God's love and action in the world of human relationships. For Christians, such a presence is embodied in the life and ministry of the historical Jesus who became for the world the Christ of faith.

I suggest that the genuine sharing of God's love, that is, the unconditional and incarnational love revealed contextually by the historical Jesus, is an intercultural, interpersonal, conversational dynamic between all cultures: religious and non-religious. For Christians, the seeds of God's love, preached and embodied by the historical Jesus, who, for Christians, became the Christ of faith, exist in all cultures and religious perspectives. The pastoral task is to discover and observe manifestations of God's vision or realm within every culture and religion. For example, for Muslims God's dominion is everywhere and is revealed through the prophet Mohammed (Peace be upon Him). In the sacred Qur'an God (Allah) speaks of a dominion of peace, love and dignity for all. Likewise, within the other religions of the world, the passion for transcendence, life, truth, friendship and meaningful belonging are reflected for humanity in different ways.

God's agenda for humankind is unconditional love, forgiveness and life-giving belonging. In various ways different cultures and religions reflect this agenda. The evolving religious constructions of meaning handed down from generation to generation engage the temporal and spiritual characteristics of human life in its struggle to find worthwhile meaning and purpose. These meaning structures embodied in symbols, i.e. persons, texts, sacraments, institutions, rituals, creeds and so on, give shape to a life-giving pastoral presence. The cross for Christians is a powerful symbol of God's suffering presence. It is a reminder to us that God holds us and loves us in our suffering turmoil and is in faithful solidarity with us going through every inch of suffering. It does not end there. Our Christian tradition celebrates the resurrection that follows during Easter. We believe that we will rise again and live forever. For example, our liturgies have the potential to help us construct life-giving meaning and reflect the presence of God. Simply lighting a candle in a church can connect us to something greater than ourselves. Such meaning constructions enable people to communicate, educate and form significant perceptions of themselves as well as shape an understanding of an Ultimate reality such as God. For Christians, the significance and purpose of life, understood in the context of the Reign of God proclaimed by Jesus, provides a powerful foundation for hope in the face of suffering, illness and death. For others, different symbols and foundations of hope will connect them to the transcendent and to the meaning of their suffering.

My own theology of ministry is grounded in the metaphor of incarnation. God empathised so much with our humanness that God became one like us. God wanted to be so present to us that this presence became concretised and symbolised in the historical Jesus who became the Christ of faith. Some practitioners of ministry may want to use the language of the Trinity as another helpful way to understand the relationality of ministry. Highlighting the importance of relationship as the receptacle for human transformation, John Patton observes that:

> Rediscovering one's self and one's power to live and to change in the context of relationship is what pastoral care is all about. Care is pastoral when it looks deeper than the immediate circumstances of a person's life and reminds that person that he or she is a child of God created in and for relationship.[11]

Assisting people in coming to understand that they are children of God may be difficult, especially when the suffering other is in a painful space. Do I, as a caregiver, have a sense that I am a child of God in my own ministry to the broken and fragile patients, clients and parishioners? What is my sense of incarnational theology? How is God made concrete in my own life? Whatever the answers are to these questions, I need to reflect a genuine embodiment (presence) and be a visible witness to the Christian faith I profess. That is to say, the minister needs to walk the talk of Christian faith. Ministry is not an occasion for proselytising for a particular faith, especially to those who are most vulnerable because of loss, illness, relationship breakdown, imprisonment or bereavement. Should this happen then we create a hostage situation for the patient or family. This action would not reflect the God Jesus knew.

GOD'S PRESENCE IN JESUS

God coming into the human world as a fragile little infant teaches us about a God who is interested in the fragility of every human person. Exploring the biblical texts and trawling through the gospels can be an enlightening exercise to build a case for effective pastoral care. How is God present in a meaningful way to us in our daily lives? What does that presence look like and how do we recognise and know it?

Jesus' ministry illustrated God's presence and action in the world of his time. This was service toward the Reign of God. Jesus was a visible expression of the Reign of God. He did not so much come to talk about himself as to help his listeners grasp the notion of God's reign: how this reign was shaped and where it could be found. Jesus' words and actions reveal the nature of God and the nature of Jesus' ministry. We get a glimpse of a God whose face is Jesus and whose face is also revealed in the people that Jesus came to serve. This is a God who includes those who are marginalised by general society, a God who breaks down cultural and religious taboos, a God who heals people broken-hearted from relationships gone wrong, whose dreams have been dashed and who have lost hope in their own potential for life. The incarnation of God in a human person like Jesus offers hope to a fragmented and broken world. Helping people grasp that hope is a task for the pastoral agent. This was the very presence of God to the people around him and beyond. Jesus' ministry was the manifestation of the very presence and action of God.

Jesus' presence to various people and their presence to him provide us with a particular lens to explore our own sense of presence to those on the fringes of life. As the manifestation of God's presence, Jesus gave us the example of how to be visible expressions of God's presence through our ministry at this time of salvation history. See especially Lk 4:18-19 and Mt 25:34-46 where Jesus in both these passages reveals powerfully the specifics of God's reign. Jesus exuded a prevailing spiritual presence.

We interpret God's presence and action in our lives through the words and actions of Jesus in the gospels. Jesus healing the ten lepers, his sermon on the mount, his instructions to the disciples, his chastisement of the Pharisees, and his storytelling in the parables all reveal a glimpse of the unconditional love and forgiveness of the God that Jesus knew. We are reminded of his presence on the cross and the type of presence that those under the cross were for him in his agony. This is what God is like and the particular relationship that God envisioned for the world of humanity and the created environment. When Jesus withdrew to rest and pray, he was still present. We learn that to withdraw to pray and rest is also about establishing effective presence because we are always in relationship. Relationships have been established in our ministries. These relationships have to be nourished by prayer and rest in order to engage fully again and to enhance the quality of our ministry. Perhaps by our frequent prayer and reflection our intuitive sense of who God is for us and how God heals those around us can be sharpened. The culture we live in can offer glimpses of God as well as offer life-restricting characteristics of meaning-making. However, culture can be a communicative lens through which we can discover aspects of God's revelation and God's loving/saving presence among us.

INTERCULTURAL AND INTERRELIGIOUS COMMUNICATION

What does authentic presence look like in different cultures and religious experiences? Fundamentally, presence looks the same in different cultures in the sense that there is a universality about it. However, a pastoral presence is going to be perhaps expressed differently for it to reach the deeper structures of meaning in the patient or parish or school. In order to do this, human intuition and imagination play an important part in a multicultural ministry – the ability to perceive profoundly what is going on for someone else in their space.

The construction of meaning through culture and religion becomes a basis for dialogue and conversation, which are grounded in how life informs faith and faith informs life. Through mutual respectful dialogue the reality of any form of spiritual and emotional terror is diminished or lessened and the sense of trust restored. Intercultural dialogue and communication characterised by mutual respect and reverence is essential for all to live in peace and to advance the dignity of all persons everywhere. Conversation that is focused on creating a space for a pastoral presence fosters the growth of the Reign of God in our world.

In relation to intercultural communicative interaction, communicator and educator Stella Ting-Toomey in her book *Communicating Across Cultures* suggests that: 'Mindful intercultural communication emphasises the appropriate, effective and satisfactory negotiation of shared meanings and desired goals between persons of different cultures.'[12] I claim that the transformation of personal, religious, cultural and pastoral identity occurs through the interrelational dynamics of an interreligious and intercultural encounter. I have learned from my pastoral ministry experiences in different places around the world that a flexibility of cultural and religious mindset is essential. Such a mindset needs to reflect a movement toward understanding authentic, flexible and inclusive religious identity from other cultural and faith perspectives. For example, in my ministry among the Turkana in Kenya, there was a special clay called emunyen, which people smeared over their faces to ward off evil spirits. This clay was used to anoint, as with the oil we use to anoint. Using the leaves of the Esekon tree to sprinkle water upon people as a blessing at the beginning of the celebration of the Eucharist is important for the Turkana because these green leaves symbolise life. The Esekon tree survives in the desert as its roots go at least thirty feet deep into the ground. Stella Ting-Toomey reminds us that 'mindful intercultural communication requires that we support others' desired self-concepts, including their preferred cultural, ethnic, gender and personal identities'.[13] Intercultural contact is not new. It has its roots deep in history when cultures and religious world views began to engage and interact with one another because of trade, war, crusade, colonisation and so on. This kind of interculturation brought division and reinforced exclusion. Interculturation today needs to be mindful of just how vulnerable we all are in a local and global society and that cultural and religious inclusion is essential to our human survival into the future. The words we use can either hurt or heal. Jesus in his own communications used words that encouraged some, challenged some and healed others. The use of words was important. We need to use them carefully and with good intention in our ministry and especially in the theology that we construct.

Though there are many examples of intercultural and interreligious encounters from a Christian viewpoint in Scripture, the narratives of Jesus challenging the Pharisees and Sadducees reminds us of how difficult it can be to transform embedded religious mindsets, especially when these are linked to a particular exclusive personal and religious identity. The Pharisees were challenged to expand their personal and communal horizon of spiritual vision. If they could have let go of their embedded fears they would have experienced the freedom of a more expanded and liberating religious and spiritual identity. They might have discovered something more about both the transcendent and immanent presence of God in their very midst.

The presence and engagement of Jesus with many different people of his time, and the contrasting context of our time highlights specific perspectives into and understandings of an interreligious presence for empathy and healing within diverse cultures. The particular ways of knowing and being in the world that define who the participants are within these contexts and how they interact with culture on their own terms undergird the process of discovering and observing aspects of the 'unknown' God. Seeing and appreciating the characteristics of an ultimate reality (God) that has not yet been met or encountered can be exciting and challenging, and can offer life-giving opportunities for those with a capacity for embracing contrasting images of that ultimate reality. I certainly experienced this within parishes and hospitals as well as in the classroom. For example, the Turkana word for God is Akuj. Was this the same God that Jesus knew? Conversation with the Turkana may help answer this question. This leads me to suggest briefly some basic principles for a meaningful conversation/dialogue to enhance a quality presence among those we are invited to serve, to care for and to encourage.

PRINCIPLES FOR FOCUSED AND MEANINGFUL CONVERSATION FOR LIFE-GIVING PRESENCE

Life-giving pastoral presence depends upon a genuine mutually respectful dialogue. Such dialogue aims at coming to terms with divergent views and incongruities that inevitably do emerge in relation to ministry. Everyone has a particular faith perspective, cultural symbol, religious sensibility and personal story. When some people disagree and perhaps refuse to assent to particular decisions, they must always know that their particular faith perspective or 'world view' is incorporated into the overall process for dialogue to make effective decisions. This dialogical method of discourse ensures the continuance of good will as well as creating the necessary consensus for change toward authentic pastoral presence development within contemporary culture. Undergirding any dialogue related to effective pastoral presence and relevant meaning-making must be the inner capacity on the part of all ministers engaged in the process to evaluate information and examine current trends critically. That is to say, the 'life-world'[14] in which ministers live must be critically evaluated for meaning and a sense of identity. Since ministers come from different backgrounds, the understanding of who they are as individuals and who they are as a community of believers within diverse life-worlds becomes clearer through a dialectical or focused conversation. Who the ministers are within their own family systems, workplaces, organisations and institutions can help them in reflecting upon relevant spiritual symbols to express their sense of faith and the meaning of their lives. Educating and forming ministers to listen attentively and reflectively to the various stories, guiding myths, memories and interests of others is crucial within the conversation for effective pastoral presence. The process requires intentionality, commitment, acceptance, openness and goodwill among all in order to create a safe pastoral environment.

I note six principles for a dialogue of meaningful and relevant presence. Should any of these principles be overlooked, the conversation may become less than helpful. However, the fact that pastoral agents ignore some principles need not be the end of the process. Efforts should always continue to keep the conversation alive by noting the difficulties. Avoid the blame game. Always remember that dialogue is never easy, even among adherents of the same religious world view. Here are my suggestions: (1) It is crucial to listen in order to hear the other. (2) A solid conviction in one's own religious or non-religious world view is necessary. (3) Respect for the other even if one disagrees is vital. (4) Engage in kenosis, whereby one empties out prejudice, self-righteousness and intellectual arrogance. (5) Engage in conflict in a respectful pastoral manner. There will be inevitable conflict – have a way of dealing with it appropriately both personally and communally. (6) Accept and respect those who are 'different' – pray together in each others' places of worship. Share your faith, your hope (in order to understand the mean-making associated with each other's faith tradition). As practical theologian Maryanne Confoy states:

> We continue, throughout our lives, wherever we are in our mystical journey of living and loving, to discover things about

ourselves, our family and our society that it would be easier not to know. But in the knowing comes a new understanding, and in the understanding comes forgiveness, and from forgiveness flows compassion – the expansive God-given love – that reaches beyond the boundaries of our own pain and self-interest to others.[15]

For example, various ways of prayer, meditation, rituals within our pastoral contexts can help us move from mere tolerance to acceptance and appreciation of other structures. Pastoral agents need to understand why people pray or meditate in these contexts. These are the principles for an intercultural encounter that desires peace, acceptance, appreciation of each other and a life-giving community. Linked to this insight is the role that every culture and religion plays as important resources in the discovery and practice of an authentic intercultural non-anxious presence.

INTERCULTURAL PASTORAL CARE

Intercultural pastoral care and ministry involves sensitivity and understanding of other people living out of different cultural and religious world views. Such a dynamic does not alienate or threaten one's own world view. Rather, such interaction only enhances and broadens the minister's own limited view of the world. I name this process of human interaction between cultures and religious perspectives 'interculturation'.[16]

Interculturation is a relational process of meaningful pastoral presence between two or more people in a specific historical context, happening between every minister/caregiver and client, patient, or parishioner toward the humanisation of both. To be an intercultural minister/caregiver offering an effective pastoral presence to those who are 'other' is to be cognisant that one's own ministerial identity is not dependent upon the externals of culture. The intercultural person is not outside culture, which would indicate that somehow it is possible to stand outside one's humanity. Rather, being aware of one's own cultural assumptions allows the minister to assest his/her unique identity with the accretions of a particular culture. The reason for this is that the caregiver can be freer to minister cross-culturally.[17] Consequently with this understanding of crossing cultural boundaries, ministers need to perceive the impact this kind of presence has on their sense of who they are and their feeling of inner freedom for themselves and others around them.

CONCLUSION

The capacity to be authentically present to another person(s) is challenging for every caregiver. Pastoral ministers specifically are challenged to refine the skills necessary in order to create a life-giving safe space for spiritual nurturance and support. Learning to be present to the uncomfortable nature of suffering and dying can be a great gift to someone terminally ill or experiencing life as hopeless. This presence is more than just being physically present. It means being attuned and sensitive to the other suffering person. Suspending one's own need for care, recognition and attention as pastoral agent in the moment is very important. This is where appropriate personal, cultural and religious boundaries need to be observed. The self-care of the minister requires another safe and life-giving space separate from the immediate ministerial context. The role of silence is important and the capacity to be comfortable with silence is crucial for the minister. Silence can facilitate and foster an atmosphere of trust, safety, intimacy, for life-giving relationship, where a space for fruitful sharing and a feeling of 'belongingness' can occur between two or more persons. In silence people can be present to each other in a profound way. In the mix is vulnerability as an essential element in ministry in every cultural or religious context. Whiteside notes that 'Vulnerability is vital to a ministry that is truly human and sensitive. Ministers are at their best when they are in touch with the fragility and shadow in their lives'.[18] Paradoxically, this is the location for genuine redemption and actual hope. Pope Benedict XVI reminds us in his 2007 encyclical *Spe salvi*:

Redemption is offered to us in the sense that we have been given hope, trustworthy hope, by virtue of which we can face our present: the present, even if it is arduous, can be lived and accepted if it leads towards a goal, if we can be sure of this goal, and if this goal is great enough to justify the effort of the journey (1).

QUESTIONS FOR REFLECTION

I. What is your understanding of an effective pastoral presence and pastoral identity?

II. In what ways will pastoral theology need to evolve so that the loving presence of God in Jesus Christ is represented in Ireland and beyond?

III. How do different cultural and religious viewpoints impact on your ministry context?

NOTES

1. *Eternal Echoes: Exploring Our Hunger to Belong*, New York: Harper Perennial, 2000, p. 99.

2. *Anam Cara: A Book of Celtic Wisdom*, New York: Harper Collins, 1998, p. 137. For a detailed account of different kinds of presence, see also *Eternal Echoes*, pp. 52–99.

3. See John Patton, *Pastoral Care: An Essential Guide*, Nashville: Abingdon Press, 2005, p. 22.

4. O'Donohue, *Anam Cara*, p. 199.

5. See O'Donohue, *Eternal Echoes*, p. 55.

6. Ibid.

7. *Pedagogy of Freedom: Ethics, Democracy, and Civic Courage*, Maryland: Lanham: Rowman & Littlefield Publishers, 1998, pp. 25–6.

8. See Patricia O'Connell Killen and John de Beer, *The Art of Theological Reflection*, New York: Crossroad Publishing Company, 1994, 1997, p. 45.

9. See Bob Whiteside, 'The Art of Pastoral Ministry' in *The Furrow*, Vol. 59, No. 7/8 (2008), p. 399.

10. See John Patton, *Pastoral Care: An Essential Guide*, p. 26.

11. Ibid., p. 30.

12. New York/London: The Guilford Press, 1999, p. 21.

13. Ibid., pp. 21–2.

14. The 'life-world' of every person is the meaning perspectives or world view in which they are always situated, that is, sociolinguistic, epistemic, psychological, religious and cultural.

15. See Maryanne Confoy, 'Mysticism – God's Initiative and Our Response' in Thomas H. Groome and Harold Daly Horell (eds), *Horizons and Hopes: The Future of Religious Education*, New York/Mahwah, NJ: Paulist Press, 2003, p. 130.

16. See Thomas G. Grenham, *The Unknown God: Religious and Theological Interculturation*, Bern, Switzerland: Peter Lang Publishing, pp. 63–87.

17. For a detailed discussion on identity change and intercultural adaptation, see Stella Ting-Toomey, op. cit., pp. 233–60.

18. See Bob Whiteside, 'The Art of Pastoral Ministry', p. 404.

CHAPTER THREE

THE PASTORAL CONTEXT AS A LIVING SYSTEM: IMPLICATIONS FOR THEOLOGY AND PRACTICE

Anne Codd

Over the last five years, I have worked as a tutor/facilitator for the Pastoral Department of the Milltown Institute, and in a variety of other settings in this country and elsewhere. For the most part the modules and assignments in which I am involved relate to leadership, collaboration and participation in the life, mission and ministry of Christian faith communities. In a variety of groups and settings, participants and I have shared our *Gaudium et spes*, the joy and hope – the grief and anguish too – which arise as we engage pastorally in richly diverse cultural and social contexts. While holding open the vision of Church which shines through our ecclesiological studies, we have also articulated the dilemmas of institutionalism in its various manifestations.

Against this background we are discovering the liberating, empowering and also challenging possibilities of a Living System approach to interpretation and action in personal, communal and ecclesial settings. In this, we harvest the inherent dynamism which we find in the interplay of imagination and experience, of the mystical and the historical, of the aesthetic and the organic.

I welcome this opportunity to offer this 'account of the hope that is in me'. I am aware that in addressing this topic I am touching upon wide-ranging and ongoing theological conversations. The theoretical foundations for a Living System approach to the pastoral context which I have found most useful lie in communion ecclesiology, in particular as I seek interfaces between it and an open-system perspective on organisations in context of quantum thinking.

I must clarify at this point that I am not here seeking an application of Living System Theory, as in the seminal work of James Grier Miller (1978),[1] to our theology of Church, though this might indeed be a worthwhile exercise. My attention is drawn rather, as the title indicates, to the totality of the context within which the Church lives, which it shares and where it fulfils its mission. I want to explore the implications for ecclesiology and for ecclesial practice of taking a systemic view of that context.

I wish to acknowledge from the outset the contribution of several groups and individuals within the learning community at Milltown and elsewhere to the evolution of this chapter. The exercise of interrogating our images and self-understanding as faith communities in our present-day contexts, and of opening ourselves to paradigmatic shifts in this regard, has been at times challenging, at times exciting, always engaging. The convergence of method and message has often been quite remarkable.

I know that we are not the first or only explorers in this territory. The essential relationality of ecclesial communities, for example, is implicitly accepted in discussions of Church life at all levels. The current realities of globalisation and climate change unequivocally attest to deep interconnectedness between seemingly disparate elements and discrete systems in our universe. It is also widely accepted that mechanistic descriptions of organisations in general provide inadequate means for dealing with the variety and variability of the human factor, which is especially operative in the multicultural contexts in which we live today. However, though we subscribe intellectually to current orientations towards personalist, holistic and provisional world views, there is still, in the operations of pastoral life, much that is overly functional, fragmented and uncertain. It is these dichotomies that feature centrally in my work. It is not acceptable, in my view, to interpret inconsistencies between theological vision and pastoral practice as inevitable manifestations of the divine-human character of Christian communities.

As I continue to explore a Living System approach in pastoral theology, I and others with me experience refreshment of spirit, a sense of significance and self-belief, and ultimately of real responsibility. From these come renewed commitment to engage in our Church as both institution and community.

COMMUNION ECCLESIOLOGY

After the Council of Trent (1545–1563) the self-understanding of the Catholic Church was predominantly (if not exclusively) juridical and its vision of itself was largely that of a 'perfect society' – *societas perfecta*.[2] As M-J le Guillou observes:

> [T]he notion of society ... led to a static conception of the Church as a fully-formed juridical institution, standing outside time, and resulted in the practical disappearance of the whole dynamic vision of the Church as the instrument of a plan of universal and cosmic dimensions.[3]

The motif of the perfect society was preserved in official ecclesiology right up to the publication of the encyclical of Pius XII, *Mystici corporis*.[4] Nevertheless, *Mystici corporis* endorsed for its time the use of an organic image from the scriptures, so that, as Emmanuel Lanne observes, it may indeed be said to have marked a 'point of arrival and a point of departure' in the official teaching of the Church.[5]

Walter Kasper locates the emergence of communion ecclesiology within the biblical, liturgical, patristic and pastoral revival which took place in the first half of the twentieth century. He recognises the desire for new forms of community already present in the rising generations following the collapse of European society with World War I. Twenty years after Vatican II, Kasper identified similar movements in western society – people in search of participation and solidarity, while subjecting large-scale institutions, including the Church, to 'considerable scepticism'.[6]

Writing in 1989, Kasper observes:

> ... one of the guiding ideas of the last council – perhaps *the* guiding idea – was ... *communio* – communion. By taking this as a leitmotif, the council succeeded in uncovering one of the deepest questions of the time, refining it in the light of the gospel, and answering it in a way that took it beyond a purely human questioning and seeking.[7]

Twenty years on, in the unquestionably more globalised context of today, the search for human community goes on apace. Among believers this quest manifests itself everywhere that Church leaders engage in consultation and pastoral planning. The findings of recent diocesan listening processes here, for example, invariably call for a Church that is a community in which to belong, a place of nurture along the road of life and of support in times of need, with a culture of invitation and welcome, especially for the young and the stranger, and a system of organisation marked by communication and consultation, equality and empowerment.

Vatican II presents three fundamental aspects of communion as a characteristic of Christianity: (1) the basis of all communion is the familial relationship with God to which we are invited in fulfilment of our creation in God's image and likeness; (2) this communion has been realised in a unique way in history through the incarnation – 'Jesus Christ is the quintessence of all communion between God and human beings';[8] and (3) it is the Holy Spirit, dwelling in the Church and in the hearts of believers, who forms the Church into a 'unity of communion with God and among its own members'.[9]

A first point of critique of much ecclesial conversation, planning and practice arises from this foundational understanding of communion ecclesiology. The divine invitation to communion, cradled in our very creation in the divine image, cannot be appropriated by Christian believers as a privilege of theirs over-against all others. The Church as a 'home and school of communion' is not gifted with participation in the divine life for its members alone, but for the whole of humanity, in all its cultural and religious diversity. The aspiration of a hospitable, inclusive Church is legitimate, but it is also challenging. An enclave of the like-minded is not community. Rather, authentic community is inseparable from mission. This point will arise later, as corroborated in a Living System approach.

The origins of modern catholic communion[10] ecclesiology are ascribed to J.A. Mohler. Mohler understands the Church as primarily a community that enjoys communion with God and one another through Jesus and the Spirit. He sees the Church evolving from the love that was shared between Jesus and his disciples. In his context, Mohler makes clear that understanding the Church in personal and communal terms is much more than a counterpoint for either individualistic pietism or juridical institutionalism. Neither is Mohler's insistence on the historical nature of the Church and its grounding in human experience to be interpreted as due solely to the culture of the Enlightenment.

Mohler claims that tradition is an essential complement to scripture, and that the patristic sources, including their reflection on the early communities' experience of being Church, are integral to revelation. It is no surprise, therefore, that he upholds – especially in his early work – the structures which developed organically in the first three centuries, including the world-wide episcopacy and the papacy, as expressions of deep unity in the Spirit (not without diversity), and as of the essence of the Church. In this, Mohler counters the anti-supernaturalism of modernity, and can arguably be said to prefigure the 'hierarchically ordered communion' of later ecclesiology, including that of Vatican II. The highest representation of the Church unity is, for Mohler, the Eucharist, and the image that best describes the Church is the Body of Christ.

Mohler's ecclesiology has significant points of comparison with his contemporary, Schleiermacher. However, Mohler insists – against protestant legitimations of division – that the unity of the Church contains in itself all antitheses. This view is deeply resonant with core tenets of systems theory.

For Mohler, to say that the Church is trinitarian is much more than symbolic – rather, the Trinity is revealed in the experience in the Church of relationship with God and one another in Christ, an experience which is enabled by the Spirit. Life in the Church reflects the life of God in God's own inner existence. In his later writing Mohler was careful to go beyond any interpretation of the Church life which could obliterate either the transcendence of God (experienced as the action of God's Spirit) or human freedom (expressed through willing conformity to Christ). In this way, he grappled with and progressively held in dynamic distinction and interrelation the human and divine elements of Church.

From even this cursory overview, it is clear that Mohler's contribution to catholic ecclesiology is much more than polemic. The enduring value of his work rests on its deep roots within the founding story of the Christian tradition, on its identification of Eucharist as the highest expression of communion with God and unity among believers, and on his use of the Pauline image of the body of Christ to describe his organic view of the Church. His relevance to this exploration of a Living System approach to the pastoral context is his ongoing search for balance in the self-understanding of Church, partaking as it does of divine mystery and existing as it does historically in time and space.

Yves Congar, acknowledged as a major influence in Vatican II,[11] identifies Mohler as a source which he directly used. For Congar, the existence of the Church in history is integral to what the Church is, and to that extent he may be said to be in close continuity with the early Mohler. Congar pursued his interrogation of Church and Church reform with uncompromising attention to its historical nature, while he always distinguished between that which is *essentially* mystical *and* historical in the Church and that which is historically conditioned and so always in need of reform. For Congar, the Church is not only present in history, but partakes of the characteristics of all historical beings. Community structures are as constitutive of Church as is its inner life. In this regard, Congar identifies a distinct role for the Holy Spirit, through enabling structural reform in the Church as it grows toward fulfilment. I will explore a little later the subtleties of correlating the activity of the Holy Spirit and the dynamics of community with the help of de Lubac's sacramental ontology.

Given his deep engagement with ecumenism, Congar championed dialogue as a way to work with diversity. This aspect of Congar's ecclesiology is highly relevant, not only to the tasks of mediation which arise within communion ecclesiology but also as a pointer to what I am working towards here – a critical review of a Living System approach to the total context of ecclesiology and ecclesial practice.

The influence of de Lubac on the ecclesiology of Vatican II is especially evident in the Council's Pastoral Constitution on the Church in the Modern World, *Gaudium et spes*. If the Church is catholic, then it is radically inclusive of all that is human. This is what supports de Lubac's claim that the Church has capacity for a 'flexible and vigorous structural unity'[12] within its paradoxical nature. The Church is at once visible and invisible, local and universal. It holds together in tensive strength its structural aspects of ordered communion with its life-missionary aspects, serving the coming of the kingdom – in which interpersonal, intercultural, interreligious conversation is not only possible but essential.

It is the essentially 'in the world' nature of Church that illuminates de Lubac's interpretation of the sacramental nature of the Church and his crystallisation of that sacramentality in the Eucharist.[13] De Lubac's Church is a church engaged in the world. As Dennis Doyle expresses it: 'It is human history which provides the arena in which Christian salvation unfolds.'[14] I find here, in the suggestion that it is necessary to take Church-in-context as the subject of ecclesiology and pastoral theology, a real incentive to pursue the Living System approach to the pastoral context.

Communion ecclesiology does not reduce Church itself to its presence in history through the ecclesial community. It does not claim that the dynamics of community constitute the totality of the workings of the Holy Spirit. Neither does communion ecclesiology treat human relationality as merely analogous to the inner life of the trinity. Rather, it sees relationship between human beings as ultimately enabled by divine activity. It suggests that Christian self-reflection yields an interpretation of our mutual loving as an expression of the life of the Trinity. Here there are shades of the later Mohler and of the sacramental ontology of de Lubac.

The vision of Church in Vatican II is that:

> ... by her relationship with Christ, the Church is a kind of sacrament or sign of intimate union with God and of the unity of all mankind. She is also an instrument for the achievement of such union and unity.[15]

Kasper stresses the critical implications of the concept of sacrament, which was requested by a number of bishops as an alternative to triumphalism, clericalism and legalism.[16] He traces its origins in the theology of Mohler and the Tubingen school in the nineteenth century, and its espousal from the 1930s onwards by de Lubac, Rahner and Schillebeeckx, among others. As used by the Council, it is always set in a Christological context. It is Christ who, through his Spirit, has made the Church the comprehensive sacrament of salvation[17] and thus brings about the union with God and the unity of humanity. The Church is a 'kind of sign or sacrament' of this salvation, and she is also an '"instrument" for its achievement'.[18]

Kasper observes that the Latin word *sacramentum* was used to translate the biblical term *mysterion*, and that it is used there in a Christological sense. As such it stands for 'that transcendent, salvific divine reality which reveals itself in a visible way [through relationship with Christ]'.[19] Both facets of Church, its relatedness through Christ to the mystery of God and its connectedness through the Spirit to the human community, are essential to what it is, neither an exclusively spiritual reality nor a solely sociological phenomenon. It is endowed by the Spirit of the risen Lord with its character and its role of continuing in the world the mission of Jesus who is the primal sacrament.

The discussions of the bishops at the 1985 Synod of Bishops provide a snapshot of the tensions in relation to the meaning and application of *communio* that arose in the aftermath of the Council. The 'synodalisation' of the Church in Germany was a serious attempt to establish structures for dialogue and collaboration. The desire, on the part of some of the German bishops, for a return to the sense of Church as *communio* was justified by them on the basis of their claim that bureaucracy was depersonalising the Church.[20] One of the advocates of this position criticised 'the many who put their hope in altering structures and conditions, whereas the Church's real renewal consists in changing of hearts and in people turning to God'.[21] Herman Pottmeyer remarks on the contrast between the German bishops, and their counterparts from the English-speaking world, and the 'Third World'. He observes the emphasis placed by Cardinal Hume on 'the concept of *communio* as an ecclesiological category, its pastoral significance in a changing society and its structural consequences; *communio*-structures should be further developed at all levels of Church life'.[22]

Pottmeyer himself acknowledges the need for a fresh sense of the spirituality of renewal. The use by the Synod of the concept of mystery to characterise the Church is, he observes, faithful to *Lumen gentium* and the Council. The development of *communio*-structures is not simply 'an emanation of autonomistic emancipation';[23] rather it is an essential element, together with the holiness of its members, in the Church's witness in a modern world.[24] In effect Pottmeyer argues that *communio*-structures do not, of themselves, threaten unity, even while addressing issues of power. Neither does a theology of Church as mystery remove the obligation that the 'visible form and organisation of the Church correspond to its ground and life-principle, i.e. the mystery of the triune God, the mystery of Jesus Christ and the mystery of the Spirit's working'.[25] 'For the Council ... there is the closest possible relationship between the Church as mysterium-sacrament and the Church as *communio*'.[26] I am motivated to pursue a systemic view of the pastoral context precisely for the potential I suspect it has to subtend this relationship and to enable its tensive strength.

John Paul II endorsed the ecclesiology and spirituality of communion as the interpretive key to his vision of Church life and mission:

> [T]he spirituality of communion, by prompting a trust and openness wholly in accord with the dignity and responsibility of every member of the People of God, supplies institutional reality with a soul.[27]

Benedict XVI, too, is keeping communion alive as a central motif:

> The love-story between God and [humanity] consists in the very fact that ... communion of will increases in a communion of thought and sentiment ...[28]

SYSTEMS

> Without systems thinking the seed of vision falls on harsh soil.
> *Peter Senge, 2005*

Having traced the evolution of communion ecclesiology and reviewed, however briefly, pointers and possibilities beyond the tensions of ideology, I will turn now to organisational theory, and in particular to the open-system perspectives on organisations emerging since the 1960s. I should mention in passing that my first real encounter with systems theory was in the context of a training programme, in 2001, at the Craighead Institute in Glasgow.[29] Craighead was then close to its roots in Ignatian discernment and the integrated approach of the Grubb Institute, London.[30] At the time, I was chairing an extensive, systematic diocesan pastoral planning process which was proving for all involved more complex and challenging than any of us had anticipated. It seemed to me even then that systemic awareness, and the attention to psychodynamics it fosters, has enormous potential to transform both interpretation and practice in this kind of work, as indeed in all pastoral ministry. I was stimulated from that time to develop, as an exercise in practical theology, the interdisciplinary dialogue which I am presenting in germ here.

I want to reiterate my conviction that organisation theory in general offers more than an array of techniques for the task of being Church. Rather, I would argue, the dialogue between systems theory and ecclesiology is a dialogue of mutual illumination and critique, a dialogue which manifests the action of God's Spirit in our shared cosmic context.

SYSTEM PERSPECTIVE ON ORGANISATIONS

W. Richard Scott of Stanford University posits three basic perspectives for the study of organisations.[31] Surveyed against the backdrop of Church viewed as an organisation, points of correlation are obvious.

(1)   A rational-system perspective which views organisation as collectivities oriented to the pursuit of relatively specific goals and exhibiting relatively highly formalised social structures. This perspective, in Scott's view, not only describes core characteristics of organisations, but presumes to establish normative structures.

(2)   A natural-system perspective which focuses attention on behaviour in organisations admits of complexity, differentiation and variability of goals and recognises the importance of informal and interpersonal structures. On this view, organisations are collectivities whose participants are pursuing multiple interests, both disparate and common, but who recognise the value of perpetuating the organisation as an important resource.

(3)   An open-system perspective which recognises that, in practice, organisations are dependent on flows of personnel, resources and information from and to their environments. Scott notes the importance of common interpretive strategies in open systems, as participants constantly seek to evaluate goals and structures and interact through several and fluid alliances. He says: 'Organisations are congeries of interdependent flows and

activities linking shifting coalitions of participants embedded in wider material-resource and institutional environments.'[32] Later, Scott observes the limitations of distinguishing between the technical aspects of environment which shape the internal work systems (those relating to tasks and goals) of an organisation, and the institutional aspects of the environment which impact on the human, political, social and cultural systems of the organisation.

The comprehensive nature of the system's interaction with its environment is the defining characteristic of the open-system perspective on organisations. 'It is precisely the throughput of nonuniformity that preserves the differential structure of an open system.'[33] From an open system point of view, there is a close connection between the *condition* of the environment and the *characteristics* of the systems within it. It follows that a complex system could not maintain its complexity in a simple environment. 'A system will exhibit no more variety than the variety to which it has been exposed in its environment.'[34] Open systems, characterised as they are by exchanges of matter and energy with their environment, can remain ordered only so long as sufficient flow of matter and energy are available.

Just as all systems are composed of subsystems, so too they exist within other, more encompassing systems. An open-system perspective requires a rationalistic, as opposed to reductionistic, approach to understanding the operations of any organisation. On this view, it is as important to look outside the system of interest and to examine its context as it is to look inside the system at its component units. In summary, the comprehensive nature of the system's interaction with its environment is the defining characteristic of the open-system perspective on organisations.[35]

My interest in Systems Theory is primarily due to my intuition that it has real potential to enable ecclesial practice to give authentic expression to ecclesial theology. I was especially interested, therefore, in a presentation by Paula Downey, entitled 'Systems and

Power: Exploring the Ecology of Change' at the Céifin conference in 2004.[36] There, Downey recounts her search for the seats of power within business, politics and media. In this, she was motivated by determination to face those in power with their responsibility for the destructive influence – both social and environmental – of their organisations. Why weren't these leaders acting more decisively in response to these issues? What would persuade them to address the challenge of deep change in their organisations? To her surprise, Downey discovered that people in positions of power and influence, paradoxically, feel quite powerless in relation to the challenge of change when that challenge is seen exclusively from within a hierarchical, mechanistic view of organisations. However, she also discovered that power does not rest exclusively in hierarchies, but is distributed within the Living System within which hierarchies reside. It is precisely this distributed power that is essential in transforming organisations. Downey's very accessible paper has been helpful for me and those I work with as we explore the dynamics of local and wider faith communities, and especially the experience of powerlessness, exclusion, and/or resistance to change.

Downey distils the core tenets of systems theory for her stated purpose. She focuses in particular on Living Systems, which Miller sees as open, self-organising systems that have the special characteristics of life and interact with their environment. Living Systems, Downey observes, form themselves. It is multiple flows of information which help life to organise itself. In human systems information includes actions, behaviours and choices as well as data, while non-material systems form themselves through the flow of energies.

'At the heart of every system there's an identity, a story or sense of what it is supposed to become.'[37] This story at the heart of the system is the basis of order in that system and the source of its patterns. Making contact with this story is of the essence in working with a system. In my own practice of facilitation, I have an axiom: seek resolution, first, in the genesis. As Thomas Groome observes, 'remembering of the genesis can release repressed dialogue'.[38]

Downey describes it this way: 'I think we need to liberate ourselves by seeing the story that traps us.'[39]

In light of her research Downey observes that new information is essential to changing a system, that 'small amounts of information repeated over time can [move] a whole community in the direction of a new value'.[40] The system makes and remakes itself, through its response to information ('feedback'). Positive feedback amplifies new information, negative feedback dampens it. In each case, feedback influences the direction of change.

According to anthropologist Gregory Bateson,[41] the difference between the systemic working of nature, and the (characteristically) mechanical way in which humans think is a major cause of problems in organisations. Certain forms of power in organisations, as identified by Downey, demonstrate this human way of thinking. The exercise of veto to eliminate observable conflict; coercion or manipulation to influence or block out discussion; the exercise of control over agendas, ideas, and existing organisational structures such as the pattern of relationships and social arrangements: all these forms of power, which Downey groups as 'power over', operate to resist change, and consumers in wider systems collude for the same purpose. Such power-relations are preserved by the mechanical world view as essential and unassailable.

Attention to the 'circular relationship between the components and the system',[42] whereby each makes the other, is the paradigmatic shift which is required, in order to enable change. Living Systems are generated through interplay of information, ideas and meaning, i.e. energies in various forms. Energy, as we know, is not definitively shaped, not definitively ordered, but rather it shapes, orders and reorders itself in response to environmental factors and the nature and purpose of the system. In self-organising systems anything that creates a disturbance plays a crucial role in causing a system to self-organise into a new form, so making 'difference' is critical.[43] (In this connection, the role of resistance in a system is a very interesting study.) A system takes meaningful new information inside, adapts, adjusts and mutates as it moves through the feedback loops and amplifies the disturbance. So, in a system we work for change right where we are. As Downey observes, 'the quantum view explains the success of small efforts' (quite differently from the Newtonian, i.e. mechanical, view).[44] All action is both local and global, and change is not only a question of critical mass but also of critical connections.

This power, which Downey calls 'power with' and 'power within', is a property of the system and its components. The organisational structure which such power seeks is the network, and networks for change generate their own systems. They rest on the conviction that power is more a process than a thing, and that it is everywhere in the system – everyone has power, so everyone has responsibility. These involve a push towards participation and positive action. But to act constructively in the world we must connect with our deepest values and, in context of this chapter, this point brings us back to our ecclesiological quest.

THE DIALOGUE: IMPLICATIONS FOR THEOLOGY

I have claimed that the dialogue between ecclesiology and organisational theory, as all the dialogues of practical theology, is one of *mutual* illumination and critique. In light of my purpose here I will concentrate in this section on the effect of systems thinking on ecclesial self-understanding and practice. In this section and the one which follows, I will try to pick up on the pointers I identified in the previous section to the areas of correlation between communion ecclesiology and systems theory.

As I explore systems theory and the possibilities of the concept of Living Systems, the vision of Church as communion gains depth and value. The critical theological question – Church revealed and given, or Church the fruit of human desire and need – takes on a new intensity, and the great catholic construction of mutual inclusivity, our 'both/and' stance, comes into its own. The Church, extension in time of the divine presence and mission in our world, as a Christological event, is essentially mystery, essentially gift; the Church as community of those who believe and follow Jesus Christ is also essentially a historical reality. Systems thinking – recognition of the relational, cosmically interconnected and ongoing responsiveness of this historical community – leads to an appreciation of this community as more than material, as a spiritually generative reality. The creative tension between the mystical and the historical as highlighted, for example by Mohler and later by Pottmeyer reflecting on the 1985 Synod, I suggest, can fruitfully be held through attention to the context as a Living System. This grounds the experience of being Church, not just in a place of mediation, but in a place that through its supporting structures can enable resonance and amplification. Is it this experience, I ask, which ultimately encourages us to interpret the being and action of the human community as enabled by the Holy Spirit? Ultimately the mystery of the Church is a window on the mystery of God. If what God does in history is so amenable to reflection through the lens of systems thinking – an interpretive schema intuited by human intellect – then the perennial questions of theology arise: who is God? And who are we?

The Living System view of the total context, which highlights the interaction between all systems and their environments, illuminates the claim that the relationship of community and mission is inescapable and mutual. I use the image of skin to represent the boundary, i.e. the identity-forming purpose of the system. The image communicates well the inner-outer continuity of open systems. By taking a Living System perspective on the context – local, global and cosmic – of Church, I suggest that the dangers of internally-focused ecclesiology (as demonstrated in the consultation stages of pastoral planning to which I referred above) can be avoided. The inseparability of community and mission is brought into sharp focus, as are the global and cosmic reaches of that mission.

The Dialogue: Implications for Pastoral Practice

In the introduction to this chapter, I took the view that inconsistencies between vision and practice should not simply be accepted as inevitable manifestations of the paradoxical nature of the Church. I will now look at systemic approaches that I believe can address inconsistencies under the headings of: (1) the essential relationality of Church; (2) interconnectedness (internal and external) of faith communities; (3) dialogue.

TOWARDS RELATIONALITY

Separateness as a human characteristic is traced by anthropologists to our transition from nomadic to settled lifestyle, with its implication of command and control. This understanding was later compounded by the emergence of early science and its mechanistic world view. It was, arguably, further endorsed by enlightenment philosophy and the turn to the subject. Our challenge, at this time, is to re-imagine human autonomy in light of our undeniable communality. It comes as no surprise that relational approaches are now playing an ever more important role as a method in theology.[45] What follows are merely pointers to ways in which truly relational approaches would impact on pastoral practice.

- The 2005 edition of Peter Senge's *The Fifth Discipline* is, in places, as apt as a guide to our life together in Church as to organisational learning in the world of business. Senge observes: 'When managers are committed to growing people ... or committed to using conversation as the core process of change, their practices reflect ... our innate desire to grow as human beings and to be in relationship with one another.'[46]

- Systems thinking highlights the need for consistency between the structures of an organisation and its purpose. A Living System view of the pastoral context evokes Church structures that are participative, and that give visible expression, in each local cultural context, to our ecclesiology. The scope for developing these structures, even within present Church discipline, has by no means been exhausted.

- The roles which members assume in organisations are, in systemic terms, inseparable from the relations and responsibilities which connect persons-in-role with co-actors in the system. The uniqueness of persons leads in turn to individuality in how they construct their roles, for example, in leadership, in ministerial teams and in pastoral councils. It follows that there is need for ongoing reflection and sharing of experience (a form of feedback) on the impact of new configurations of role on the mission of the organisation.

- Liturgical practice has been a focus of renewal in Church life for over forty years, and even though there is no easy consensus regarding the direction of that renewal, it is true to say that celebrations can, with imagination and effort, become highly relational. Our developing Catholic sacramental theology highlights the essential connection of ritual with life and of Eucharist with community.

- The relationality of ministry involves much more than quality in service. The personal faith and goodness of the pastoral minister is integral to the exercise and effectiveness of ministry. Quoting a colleague, Senge observes: 'The primary determinant of the outcome of an intervention is the inner state of the intervenor.'[47] Dr Thomas Grenham referred in his chapter to the role of imagination and intuition in pastoral presence especially in situations of cultural diversity. The psalmist adds: who shall climb the mountain of the Lord? The one with clean hands and pure heart (Ps 24).

- In the exercise of ministries of pastoral care, relational approaches rescue the practice from simply providing for the other's need. Authentic pastoral ministry is always mutual, enriching and empowering both those who receive and those who give. Pastoral leadership training, in my view, needs to critique seriously the servant leadership model.

- I am currently engaged by a national pastoral care agency for a project on spirituality. Until now, priest-directors in local sites have been seen as the main custodians of spirituality, and the ones at hand for ritual services. Now, in transition, rather than simply design a role for a lay person as a sort of second-best to the ordained, what this organisation – in its wisdom – is doing is in keeping with a Living System approach. Over a set period of time, the spirituality of the members is being identified and characterised in a dialogical process. The question guiding the research team is 'how are these strengths and needs to be resourced in the days ahead?' The aim is to generate a new profile for persons whose task it will be to enable, guide and sustain the spirituality of the organisation. In this way, it is hoped, members will not be passive recipients of specialist service but rather actively engaged in mutual relationships – often across significant difference – which express, nourish and transform the spiritual life of the organisation.

TOWARDS INTERCONNECTEDNESS

A willingness to see patterns replicated throughout an organisation is a key to thinking and operating systemically. Instead of breaking things up into smaller parts, it is essential to look at the whole, the bigger picture, and observe there the patterns and the relationships which mirror, and are mirrored in, the system under review.

- In an extended piece of action research, in which I was involved throughout 2003, I and my colleagues in the project tested seriously the potential of a systemic approach to parish development. The following emerged as key factors contributing to the sustainability of that development: (1) new growth has its roots in the stories and the current real situations of the parish; (2) the vision for the parish has the whole faith-community, local community and wider society in sight; (3) transformation is enabled through processes, which in the context we defined as experiential pathways (such as remembering, conversation, imaging, guided meditation) designed with purpose; and (4) structures are used to support emergent life. When we presented this work at a national pastoral conference, the response of practitioners there could be summarised as follows: this is intuitive and self-evident, but our practice falls down on almost all counts!

- Systemic thinking and systemic awareness suggest that it is impossible to transform in a sustainable way subsystems – groups or sections – within a parish while passing over others because they are, perhaps, too complex or indeed too delicate. Youth ministry, for example, is often an isolated endeavour, but cannot in fact be exercised independently of a community which welcomes young people. Neither can it be developed in the absence of some form of pastoral plan involving the whole parish.

- Neither new persons, groups, committees etc., no matter how skilled or gifted, nor new super-structures no matter how rational or inspired, can work to their brief, no matter how visionary, if roles and relations of existing personnel and groups are not reviewed and reconstituted in the process.

- In our time, much spirituality is individualistic, and places sometimes exclusive emphasis on personal life journeys. I am suggesting in this discussion that the task of reintegrating our spirituality and our ecclesiology can be greatly advanced through the imagery of the Living System, especially when it is accompanied by experiences which bring to consciousness and to action the deep relatedness of person and community, of ecclesia and cosmos.

- One of the most far-reaching implications of a Living System approach lies in how it calls members, as individuals and as groups, to see themselves always within the whole. In my experience, there is in our pastoral communities as well as in organisations in general an endemic tendency to fault some or all of the others for perceived or real absence of vision, cohesion and collaboration. This practice has no place within a Living System approach. If there is a problem, an inadequacy or a failing, then all members are part of the cause (it's not so easy to call it blame when we share it), and all have responsibility for finding ways to move the system forward towards greater authenticity.

Author and poet Paul Williams expresses this challenge:
We hate our enemies
to provide ourselves in advance
with excuses for possible failure

Only when we give up
the comforts of pessimism
the luxury of enemies
the sweetness of helplessness
can we see beyond our own doubts.[48]

- It is, however, reassuring to find that Senge agrees with what we know intuitively – systems-thinking alone will not lead to the lasting, far-reaching changes. For such transformation there is need for leaders who are attuned to and skilled in enabling the forward thrust of the system.

TOWARDS DIALOGUE

The self-understanding of the Christian Church is, from the earliest days, that of a teaching Church. 'To the apostles and their successors Christ has entrusted the office of teaching, sanctifying and governing in his name and by his power.'[49] I think all will agree that this teaching office is exercised, to this day, mainly in a didactic mode. However, the reception of dogma and decree are hugely influenced by the cultural context within which they are offered. Belief that the Spirit is given to the total Church is the basis of Kasper's claim that dialogue is 'the primary language' of the faith community.[50]

Jane Vella's extensive work on Living Systems approaches to adult learning and training are worth mentioning briefly here. Vella's commitment to dialogue education has its roots in the pedagogy of Paulo Freire, but she has invested a lifetime of practice and reflection in interpreting Freire through the contemporary lens of quantum thinking. In 2002, she wrote: 'It is a shock for most of us to consider a universe composed of energy that is patterned and spontaneous, the certainty of uncertainty, "both/and" thinking, and the connectedness of everything.'[51] For Vella, the interrelatedness of design and purpose is a given and an essential guide; she recognises the autonomy of the whole as more than a sum of the parts and therefore believes in the amplification of effort; the phenomenon of recurring patterns at all levels of a system, coupled with their interconnectedness, gives global perspective to her engagement with learning groups; for Vella every theory is constantly being constructed by application to new contexts, hence she sees, always, the need for provisionality; for her, only the openness of dialogue is worthy of the participants in adult learning and participation is of the essence of dialogue education – it is not just a technique: 'the observer is part of what she observes,' Vella notes, and 'we evoke the world we perceive'; dialogue education takes its effectiveness from the flow of energy of participants and therefore of the systems of which they are part.

Vella's dialogical method in education and training is replicated in discerning and planning processes around the world, where people move together to a systems approach. Recently, participants in the national pastoral conference here experienced the world-café[52] process as a very effective means of enabling dialogue between members of associations and movements in the Church and pastoral workers from parishes and dioceses around Ireland. Through real dialogue the unity of mission and diversity of gifts for life and ministry can be recognised, developed and celebrated.

POINTERS TO DEVELOPMENT

The dialogue between the Church's self-understanding, life and mission on the one hand and systems theory on the other is, I suggest, a dialogue that deserves to be developed in depth. This is a task which calls for serious action-research. Superficial analogies do no justice to the possibilities of such work.

It is important that pastoral practice be the subject of evaluative processes, in keeping with the principles of both systems theory and theology. These, in my view, include rootedness of practice in the history and current real circumstances of the context; relationality, interconnectedness, attention to the whole; openness to change and processes which enable transformation; and appropriate levels and styles of structure.

There is much scope for enlarged reflection and enhanced practice in contemporary processes such as: (1) reframing our ecclesiology in light of new cosmology, represented by publications such as *The Holy Web, Church and the New Universe Story*, by Cletus Wessels OP[53] and (2) reframing our sacramental theology, as in *The Cosmos as the Primary Sacrament* by Dorothy McDougall.[54]

CONCLUSION

Is there a way to image Church which will hold in a dynamic unity both its mystical nature as a community gifted with the life of the trinity and its historical nature as a human organisation unfolding in response to the Living System of the here and now? Is there an image which might capture the interrelatedness of the aesthetics of life and the organics of structure?

The closest I have come to such an image is that of the dance. Dance has the power to impact performer and audience alike; dance cannot happen unless there is a dancer, and (in a real sense) dance is not complete without a participating community. The bone and sinew of the dancer are scarcely, if ever, the focus of attention in the performance and reception of the dance, yet without these there would be no expression of dream or mood, no communication of life. The dance itself is the dancer's purpose, but it is the intentionality of mind and movement of limb which actualises it in practice. The ultimate fruit, in the total context of dancer, dance and community, is an aesthetic experience reaching beyond itself to God knows where.

QUESTIONS FOR REFLECTION

I. What resonances, if any, do you find between your own experience and the dilemmas that are explored in this chapter?

II. What aspects of a Living System approach, if any, engaged your interest so that you would wish to develop them in support of your own life mission?

III. What points from the chapter would you wish to affirm? Critique? What would you like to see researched further?

NOTES

1. James Grier Miller, *Living System*, New York: McGraw-Hill, 1978.

2. The term is used in the sense that it is 'subordinate to no other and lacks nothing required for its own institutional completeness'. A. Dulles, *Models of the Church*, New York: Doubleday, 1974, p. 31. Dulles points out the origin of the concept of *societas perfecta* in the ecclesiology of Robert Bellarmine. Rahner characterises the *societas perfecta* as 'an organisation founded by Christ, with its offices and ministries, hierarchically structured and jurisdictionally empowered', 'Theology of the Parish', in H. Rahner (ed.), *The Parish: From Theology to Practice*, Westminister, Maryland: Newman Press, 1958, p. 26.

3. 'Church', in K. Rahner (ed.), *Encyclopedia of Theology, a Concise Sacramentum Mundi*, London: Burns and Oates, 1975, pp. 215–216.

4. Pius XII, *Mystici corporis* (1943), 98.

5. E. Lanne, 'The Local Church: its Catholicity and Apostolicity', in *One in Christ* (6), 1970, pp. 295–6.

6. W. Kasper, *Theology and Church*, London: SCM Press, 1989, p. 149.

7. Ibid., p. 150.

8. Ibid., p. 152.

9. Ibid., p. 152.

10. John Paul II, *Novo millennio ineunte*, 43.

11. See 'This Church That I Love: Essays Celebrating the Centenary of the Birth of Yves Cardinal Congar', *Louvain Studies,* 29 (2004), pp. 3–4.

12. D. Doyle, *Communion Ecclesiology*, NY: Orbis Books, 2000, p. 61, quoting de Lubac, *Catholicism*, p. 152.

13. Ibid., p. 66.

14. Ibid., p. 68.

15. Vatican Council II, Dogmatic Constitution on the Church, *Lumen gentium* [hereafter LG], (1965), 1.

16. *Theology and Church*, p. 113.

17. See LG, 48.

18. See LG, 1.

19. *Theology and Church*, p. 118.

20. See 'The Church as Mysterium and as Institution' [hereafter 'Mysterium'], *Concilium*, 1986/6, pp. 99–109. "'... The ecclesiastical apparatus obscures the Church as mysterium. That is why so many young people leave the Church and go to the sects which flourish among the young". This is Cardinal Meisne's analysis.' 'Mysterium', p. 100. 'It is essential ... to put forward the Church as mysterium, transcending itself towards Christ. The synod cannot make the

distribution of power its primary topic.' Cardinal Ratzinger, quoted in 'Mysterium', ibid.

21. Cardinal Hoffner, quoted by Pottmeyer, 'Mysterium', ibid.

22. 'Mysterium', p. 101.

23. Ibid.

24. Ibid., pp. 102–3.

25. Ibid., p. 104.

26. Ibid.

27. John Paul II, *Novo millennio ineunte*, 44.

28. Benedict XVI, *Deus caritas est*, 17.

29. www.craighead.org.uk.

30. www.grubb.myzen.co.uk.

31. W.R. Scott, *Organisations, Rational, Natural, and Open Systems* (fifth edition), New Jersey: Prentice Hall, 2003.

32. Ibid., p. 29.

33. Ibid., p. 89.

34. Ibid., p. 91.

35. This point begs a conversation with Robert Schreiter on constructing local theologies.

36. P. Downey, *Global Aspirations and the Reality of Change, how can we do things differently?* Dublin: Veritas, 2004, pp. 82–105. For one description of systems thinking as it can be applied to organisational development and learning, see www.dya.ie.

37. Ibid., pp. 88–9.

38. 'Shared Christian Praxis: a Possible Theory/Method of Religious Education', in J. Astley and L. Francis (eds), *Christian Perspectives on Christian Education*, Leominster: Gracewing, 1994, p. 227.

39. Downey, op. cit., p. 103.

40. Ibid., p. 89.

41. Ibid., p. 90.

42. Ibid., p. 97.

43. Ibid., p. 98.

44. Ibid., p. 100.

45. See Leuven, *Encounters in Systematic Theology*, 1999. 'Sacramental Presence in a Postmodern Context, Fundamental Theological Approaches' began with the fundamental and theological question of experiencing God in everyday life, and searched for plausible reflection on sacramental presence.

46. P. Senge, *The Fifth Discipline, the Art and Practice of the Learning Organisation*, New York: Doubleday, 2006, p. 366.

47. Ibid., p. 372.

48. 'Common Sense', www.paulwilliams.com.

49. Second Vatican Council, Decree on the Apostolate of Lay People, *Apostolicam Actuositatem* 2, *Cathecism of the Catholic Church*, 873.

50. W. Kasper, *An Introduction to Christian Faith*, London: Burns and Oates, 1980.

51. J. Vella, *Learning to Listen, Learning to Teach*, San Francisco: Jossey-Bass, 2002, p. 29.

52. www.theworldcafe.org.

53. New York: Orbis, 2000.

54. New York: Peter Lang Publishing, 2003.

CHAPTER FOUR

SUPERVISION: QUALITY IN PASTORAL MINISTRY

Michael Carroll

This chapter will look in some detail at how practitioners and professionals in the helping professions, in particular pastoral ministers, look after themselves in order to effectively carry out their work. It will focus on supervision as one way of caring for self, reflecting on pastoral work and ensuring that the person behind the professional is in 'peak condition' for such demanding work.

Carl Rogers[1] was about seventy-five when he wrote: 'I have always been better at caring for and looking after others than I have been at caring for myself. But in these later years, I have made some progress.' He captured a universal issue of working with other people – it is easier to better care for other than to care for ourselves. I am not sure that the older we age, like Rogers, the wiser we get. Before reaching those happier insights of old age, many suffer from burnout, compassion fatigue, vicarious traumatisation, exhaustion and tiredness, often resulting in apathy, depression or withdrawal.[2] What a waste of human potential when no one cares for the carers, not even themselves. We would be wise to follow the advice of the airlines and adjust our own air masks first before attending to those of others.

SHARPENING THE SAW

In *The Seven Habits of Highly Successful People* (1989), Stephen Covey posits the following: suppose you were to come across a man in the woods working feverishly to saw down a tree. 'What are you doing,' you ask. 'Can't you see,' comes the impatient reply. 'I'm sawing down this tree.' 'You look exhausted. How long have you been working at it,' you exclaim. The man replies, 'Over five hours, and I'm beat. This is very hard work.' You inquire, 'Well, why don't you take a break for a few minutes and sharpen the saw. I'm sure your work would go a lot faster if your saw was sharp.' The man emphatically replies, 'I don't have time to sharpen the saw. I'm too busy sawing.'[3] It doesn't take a lot of imagination to get the point: if you make your living from sawing then it makes eminent sense to ensure that the saw is sharp.

Skovholt,[4] in a book aptly entitled *The Resilient Practitioner*, picks up the same theme from a slightly different angle:

How does the opera singer take care of the voice?
The football player, the body?
The carpenter, the tools?
The professor, the mind?
The photographer, the eyes?
The ballerina, the legs?
The pastoral minister, ... what?

All the above professionals will and often do take out financial insurance so that they can be compensated should anything go wrong with the instrument of their living. What do pastoral ministers need to ensure and take care of in order to stay well, to remain in good shape for the work they do? What life and health and safety insurances are needed by them to make sure the instrument with which they do their work does not break down?

Our parents and grandparents predominantly worked using their bodies. The majority of individuals who work in the helping professions go to work with their minds, their brains, their 'selves'. If our grandparents had to look after their bodies in order to look after their professional selves, we have to ensure our 'selves' are in good working order to care for our professional selves. What are these 'selves' that need to be cared for, looked after and kept 'sharp' in order to do our jobs esffectively? If the issues facing our grandparents were physical issues, then our contemporary issues are physical, emotional, psychological and spiritual ones.

How do we care for those 'selves' so that they remain in good working order?

WHO IS RESPONSIBLE?

While we hope that others will support us, that our organisations will take seriously their responsibilities for our 'health and safety', at the end of the day we are individually responsible for how we look after ourselves. It's up to you to look after the saw because you are the saw. Your honourable 'self' *is* the saw.

We still live with the myth that the fairy godmother individual or organisation, or team or partner, or family or organisation will emerge to look after us and fulfil our needs. Organisations are incredibly bad at caring for their employees. For example, in one company I visited there was a sign that said: 'If you want to be loved, get a dog.' I come across organisations where people bemoan the fact that their employer does not care for them, appreciate them, or look after them as in days gone by. By and large, the time when our organisations or companies or institutes looked after us from the beginning of our work life to the end is gone.

People are on their own in ways that those who went before were not. If you don't look after you, don't expect your community or your group or your organisation to do so for you. Our parents and grandparents had guides to help them: doctors, clergy and churches, teachers, police. We no longer have the certainties that contact with those institutions brought. Instead we are self-determining. Zuboff and Maxmin[5] have coined the term 'psychological self-determination' to capture the challenge individuals face today, and define it as: 'A deep awareness of one's own complex individuality. It is primarily the ability to assert control over your own identity.' This is not about rampant individualism but about a keen sense of one's own identity.

Individuals want to determine their own values, make decisions for themselves and decide on their sexuality, their relationships, their careers. Zuboff and Maxmin also make the point that our institutions and organisations are ill-equipped to help us on this journey towards psychological self-determination. I worked recently with a firm of highly successful lawyers to help audit the sources of stress within their firm. A number of the partners in the firm had been absent quite often because of stress-related illness. I interviewed them all and drew up a report which could be summarised in one sentence: 'This modern, highly successful firm has no way of adapting to the individual needs of its partners.' They had no women partners; they did not cater for part-time work for partners; and they had no provision for individual time off, sabbaticals or training. A number of the individuals I interviewed told me they had reached the stage of where they would have to look after themselves and make their own arrangements for life and work, rather than rely on organisations to do this for them.

Contemporary life and complicated living (characteristic in today's world) need inner power. Resilience, inner strength and toughness are needed by those in high-risk or 'high-touch jobs'.[6] In these roles, the risk of emotional or psychological damage is high. Resilience and inner strength is needed to keep going when you hit adversity or problems. How does one become and stay resilient?

HOW TO LOOK AFTER OURSELVES
The following is a number of ways in which you can look after yourself:

- Make sure you are not in survival mode but remain in competency mode. This allows you to undertake long-term planning, be creative and imaginative and, above all, reflective. Reflection is a key method of staying strong. (Mindfulness and reflection are particularly human traits; other animals/mammals do not have this ability.)

- Ensure you have energy: find your sources of energy and use them. Energy –physical, emotional, mental and spiritual – keeps us going. Indeed, insights from sports coaching and sports psychology are increasingly being incorporated into the work life of organisations, teaching important lessons about looking after multiple energies.

- Move away from fear as a motivator. So many people are driven by their fears, many of them manufactured fears. Fear is a very costly emotion and can drive us into survival mode where fight, flight, fragment or freeze become the operational modes of life and learning.
- Reflect but don't over-reflect. Being able to reflect and learn from experience ensures we do not repeat mistakes and gives us insights into how to work more effectively. However, over-reflection impacts our lives and our work. Performance deteriorates if we ruminate on work.
- Set up support networks.
- Be self-aware – our capacity to fool ourselves is immense. Fine[7] refers to this as the vain or pig-headed brain: wonderfully adept at hiding from you that which you do not want to know.
- Use supervision as a way of monitoring your professional well-being and your work.
- Monitor motivation. Look at where from within your work emerges.[8]

To look particularly at the stress suffered by men in the workplace, compounded by the seeming inability of many to share their feelings and worries, their propensity to bottle up their feelings, and their reluctance to ask for help, last year (2008) saw many high-profile suicides in Britain, widely reported in the media. The male suicide rate in the UK is now up to four times higher than that of women. Why do we men suffer in silence; why are we reluctant to ask for help; why do we have to be so strong; why can't we face our vulnerabilities? This point is so important for ministry and for supervision in ministry. (I would very much like to see a conference on men and ministry.) Jourard writes:

> Men are difficult to love. If a man is reluctant to make himself known to another person, even to his spouse because it is not manly to be psychologically naked, then it follows that men will be difficult to love. That is, it will be difficult for a woman or another man to know the immediate present state of the

man's self and his needs will thereby go unmet. Some men are so skilled at dissembling, at seeming, that even their wives will not know when they are lonely, bored, anxious, in pain, thwarted, hungering for affection etc. And the man, blocked by pride, dare not disclose his despair or need. The fear of intimacy has held men in terrible isolation and loneliness.[9]

I often hear people say that they are not the problem. 'Out there' is the problem: materialism, or individualism, or selfishness, or lack of caring. It is others that are resistant. While I don't want to add to the burden suffered by many managers, often the problem lies with them. Some quite frightening statistics remind us that often what seems to be the solution is actually the problem: 65 per cent of people don't leave their jobs, they leave their managers. A recent book entitled *The Enthusiastic Employee*[10] surveyed 200,000 employees over twenty-six companies. The authors wanted to know why enthusiasm dipped, often only after a few months. The answer was simple: enthusiasm dipped because of the way employees were managed.

When problem-solving, we must start with ourselves. Abrashoff puts it well:

> When I could not get the results I wanted, I swallowed my temper and turned inwards to see if I was part of the problem … I discovered that 90 per cent of the time, I was at least as much a part of the problem as my people were. It's funny how often the problem is you.[11]

Many pastoral ministers are in powerful positions or positions of power, and when you are, it's difficult to think you might be the problem, or at least part of it.

Another problem is imperceptibility: we don't notice what is happening; we build up habits, bad habits, and habits are always difficult to break. The brain can be very deceptive. Strangely enough, it does not like to learn. By about eighteen years of age, it has laid down all the needed neural pathways. After that, our brains become lazy. They need prodding to get us to change our habits. The brain is a habit-forming machine, which helps when you don't need to do much thinking. However, the drawback is that, without noticing it, we end up doing things that are not helpful. We fall asleep, psychologically and emotionally, and don't even see what is going on. We wake up and ask: how did I get here. We go on automatic pilot and stop thinking of what we are doing – we churn out the same phrases and the same rituals that end up having no heart, we get caught into mindless routines that take on a life of their own. The Dinka and Nuer tribes of the Sudan have a curious tradition: they extract the permanent front teeth of their children – up to six bottom teeth and two top teeth, which results in a sunken chin, a collapsed lower lip and a speech impediment. This custom originated over a hundred years ago as a method of dealing with tetanus. Villagers started pulling out their own front teeth and those of their children in order to eat and drink.[12] The lockjaw epidemic is long past, but the Dinka and Nuer tribes still pull out their children's front teeth. Why? How easy it is to get caught into routines that were once meaningful. So often we freeze meaning and capture it as if it were to last for all time. We make it inflexible, unchangeable, and then the routines and habits kick in, like magical rituals that are supposed to work irrespective of context. When you forget context you forget humanity and mindless routine becomes the order of the day.

Often we hide behind our professional masks and jargon. It is so easy to put on the professional face and go into professional mode. Where is the person behind the professional? We use language for others not meant for ourselves; we apply treatments to them but not to ourselves; we suggest they live better lives but not us. We forget that what we teach and recommend for others we should apply to our own lives. Religious language is one of the most universal masks we can adopt. The ability to hide behind religious language is very easy.

Hiding behind our professional masks often moves us towards burnout, compassion fatigue and secondary traumatisation. We get over-involved, over-think and lose perspective. We need to stay well, stay in good condition.

SPORTS PSYCHOLOGY AND PEAK CONDITION

Let's consider the people who are good at looking after themselves: sports people. There is a lot of interesting material coming through from the fields of sports coaching and sports psychology. Some studies have been done on 'super' people – the best footballers, athletes, as well as musicians, artists etc. This research concludes that these 'super' people engage in a number of key activities that put them in this 'super' bracket:

- They practice more. We need to keep ourselves in practice all the time: keep training, keep up to date.
- They always ask for feedback. They ensure that there are people around them who will provide feedback. Often in our lives, where everyone else sees the problem, we are the last to know. It's a true friend who will give you the feedback that no one else will. But often we stay silent; we don't speak up.
- They stop and relax. We don't stop and relax enough. Sports people build up muscles by stretching them and releasing them. The difference between us and sports people is that while we stretch, we do not release. Sports psychology talks to us about four types of energy and how important they are: physical (the amount of your energy); emotional (the quality of your energy); mental (the focus of your energy); and spiritual (the source of your energy).

THE QUESTIONS BEHIND PASTORAL MINISTRY

The demands of the modern pastoral minister (priest, counsellor, youth worker, social worker, psychologist, teacher etc.) are immense:

- There is a new breed of person out there. We have various names for them (Bobos, Generation X). The bourgeois bohemians (Bobos) combine the traditional values of hard work and making money with the bohemian free spirit that flouts convention. What do they need and how do we meet those needs? How to combine modern living with spirituality?

- Ours is a multi-cultural society where different values and different lifestyles intermingle.
- There are demands in high-risk jobs, i.e. possible psychological or emotional damage, such as burnout, compassion fatigue and secondary traumatisation, to those who are seen as helpers.

In the light of these contemporary issues, how do we define pastoral ministry? It is important to know what we are doing if we call something pastoral ministry. We have used a number of other terms: pastoral care, pastoral presence, pastoral theology, pastoral practice. Is the role of the minister like that of a salesperson? Is Pastoral Theology the sales department for theology, taking principles, models and frameworks of theological thinking and applying them to individuals, groups and organisations? Whose agenda is primary or at stake when I am ministering pastorally? If I am counselling or doing supervision, I have no doubt whose agenda is central. Is the 'client' proactive or reactive when you meet with them in a pastoral ministry relationship? What is being sold?

THE BRAIN AND MINISTRY

To return to a discussion of the brain, there are three parts to our brains, or indeed three brains. The reptilian brain, the oldest brain, is what we share in common with reptiles. This brain controls basic functions such as breathing, swallowing and heartbeat. From here comes aggression and courtship: defence and mating – a pretty basic brain. Some people use only this brain and don't access or utilise the other brains. They spend their lives defending their territory without much reflection.

The second brain is called the limbic or mammalian brain and, as the name suggests, developed with the advent of mammals. Mammals differed from reptiles in that they carried their young, entering into a relationship with their offspring in ways that reptiles did not. While reptiles are quickly indifferent to their young, mammals create a relationship that is ongoing. They communicate with, they play with, they touch, they feed. Most of all they feel: they have emotional connections with their offspring.

The purpose of emotionality is now clear: to provide messengers.[13] Ekman points out that emotional expressiveness equips human beings with a sophisticated communications system.[14] It gives us access to the internal state of other people, irrespective of race or place. A child scans his mother's face to read her internal world. Often when I told people I was a psychologist, they would jokingly ask if I could read their minds. I used to reassure them I couldn't, until I realised that my limbic brain is meant to do so. You read the minds of others; you access their inner worlds through this marvellous limbic brain that is the seat of emotions, emotional connection and emotional regulation. Called limbic resonance, the limbic brain monitors and reads everything: face, body, expressions, to discover intentions. There are no words in this brain, just connections that are emotional.

We don't just monitor the internal worlds of others, and they ours, but we also adjust our own internal world to match. This is what Lewis et al[15] call 'limbic resonance', a sort of emotional attunement. Lewis and others also talk of limbic regulation. Mary Ainsworth at the University of Virginia conducted a study wherein adults were asked to look into the eyes of babies just a few weeks old without showing any emotion. The babies' initial curiosity quickly turned to anxiety, and after approximately ninety seconds, if the adult continued to withhold any reaction or communication, to distress. The limbic or mammal brain requires a constant exchange of signals, an emotional give and take. Children die if they do not have this emotional connection or attachment. Studies conducted in orphanages, or on rhesus monkeys, from the point of attachment theory say the same thing. Limbic resonance is the means to that telepathy. It is our attunement to inner states. Attachment goes to the inner core of what love means. This is where Gerhardt[16] and Goleman[17] locate the social brain or emotional intelligence. Here is where it is formed, without words. Feelings come first: rationality builds on emotion and cannot exist without it.

We often focus our ministry on the third brain, the executive brain or the human brain, without realising the importance of emotional attunement. Nothing happens, nothing changes, no human endeavour works without limbic involvement. This is vital for pastoral ministry. In ways we have never understood as graphically before, there is no ministry without limbic, emotional contact. No emotional relationship – no ministry. You can, of course, do things to people, and you can get them to do things. Persuasion, influence, even torture works. Perhaps in the past we have had to resort to other methods of conversion because limbic resonance was in such sort supply.

It is time for the brain and insights garnered from studies on the brain to impact learning, education and ministry.

EMOTIONAL CONTAINMENT

Clinical psychologists Hughes and Youngson[18] have been asking mental health users: what are the features or characteristics that you look for in a clinical psychologist. It might surprise you to know that high on the list of those features is the ability to emotionally contain. A number said that they did not share their emotions, in order to protect the psychologist. Emotional containment is very high on pastoral ministry – how to stay with the emotions. Containing emotions, staying with them and managing them, are all essential components of pastoral ministry.

Dealing with emotions is the most important aspect of life. We have seriously neglected it in religion and in life. We realise now that we make decisions emotionally; we relate emotionally; we connect emotionally. Pastoral ministry is fundamentally an emotional experience. In fact, if it isn't an emotional experience, then it degenerates into a monologue.

When I was studying theology it was an intellectual exercise, an exercise of the third brain, the frontal cortex or executive or human brain – the most recent of the brains. It was ministry from the neck up. Your body was there to carry your head around and what mattered took place in your head. Your body existed to get your head to meetings, as someone said. Ministry was for the head, as was theology – an exercise in rationality. Emotions were distractions – to be dealt with swiftly to allow a return to the rational. This is bad thinking. William James writes that: 'The intellectual life of man consists almost wholly in his substitution of a conceptual order for the perceptual order in which his experience originally comes.'[19]

THE INSIDE-OUT PASTORAL MINISTER

Ministry was often seen as what happened to other people – it was not necessarily connected to the person of the minister. According to Covey (a management consultant):

> The inside-out professional is someone whose job comes from inside. The inside-out minister knows that the beginning is always with self, not the other, that no matter how knowledgeable, skilled or competent you are, if you're 'not OK' inside then you won't 'be OK' outside.

In *The Seven Habits of Highly Effective People*, Covey talks to managers about this:

> If I try to use human influence strategies and tactics of how to get other people to do what I want, to work better, to be more motivated, to like me and each other – while my character is fundamentally flawed, marked by duplicity and insincerity – then, in the long run, I cannot be successful. My duplicity will breed distrust and everything I do – even using so-called good human relations techniques – will be perceived as manipulative. It simply makes no difference how good the rhetoric or even how good the intentions are: there is little or no trust, there is no foundation for permanent success.[20]

That is quite a statement from a management consultant talking about other managers. Who you are affects your ministry dramatically. You have to start with you. The following quote from Emerson captures the essence of this: 'What you *are* shouts so loudly in my ears that I cannot hear what you say.'[21] Covey's insight is that the message is not distinct from me, 'You *are* the message' or '*You* are the message'. We are ministry-in-action rather than functional ministers. The best principle of education is that individuals learn from what they see rather than from what they hear. We do more readily what is modelled for us rather than what others tell us to do. Research in counselling and psychotherapy show that clients move towards the health and moral values of their helpers, without them being mentioned. We lead people to where we are, without knowing it.

Inside-out ministry is about ministry as a way of life. You live the life you minister. You minister to you first of all, then to others. Living the ministerial life precedes being a helper to others in much the same way as spiritual directors have lived and been involved in what they are helping others find and discover for themselves.

Fundamental choices make the difference. You choose something, and then it comes from within you. Ministry, as I see it, is a relational concept – it involves people meeting.

- If you don't believe it, don't preach it – you are insulting me if you do.
- Share with me where you are.
- Be honest with me (I can take it).

Often we are dishonest as pastoral ministers, not sharing with others what we really think or feel or worry about, or doubt or wonder over. We become, according to Margaret Wheatley, 'Like bewildered shamans, [performing] rituals passed down to us, hoping they will perform miracles'.[22]

SUBJECTIVITY AND PASTORAL MINISTRY

Change and ministry must therefore begin with the helper and his/her subjectivity:

- In changing my thoughts, I change yours.
- In creating new hope for myself, I recreate new hope for you.
- My new vision of myself becomes the springboard for a new vision of you.

- You are not the problem, my subjectivity is. You are not the solution, my subjectivity is.

The way I think about you as my client, my supervisee, my parishioner, my spiritual directee makes you a problem or a solution, a disaster or a hope. We become what the minds and spirits of others make us just as our minds and spirits create and recreate others. When you think the problem is out there, that thought is the problem. When your client moves beyond their limitations, it must be because you are able to move beyond yours. When your client is open to learning, it is because you are open to learning. If your parishioner or supervisee gives up, maybe he or she is simply doing what you do. The parallel process in helping others says that helpers do to clients what others do to them. We hand each other our experience, we pass it on as a gift and sometimes as a burden.

If this is so, then change begins with the helper. Learning begins with the pastoral minister. Quinn puts it well: 'When we change ourselves, we change how people see us and how they respond to us. When we change ourselves, we change the world.'[23]

For me there is no substitute for personal development and intergration as the basis for ministry and indeed for any form of helping and engaging or working with people. Mearns[24] sees four basic domains of personal development:

(1) Self-structure: a willingness and preparedness to be more aware of myself as a person.

(2) Self in relationship: a willingness and preparedness to be more aware of how I relate to others, how I manage my emotions and those of others.

(3) Self in role as worker: a willingness and preparedness to look at how I minister, how I impact others, how I share power, how I open myself up to feedback.

(4) Self as learning: ongoing openness and development, continual learning, preparedness to experiment and try new ideas, risk doing things differently.

SUPERVISION AND PASTORAL MINISTRY

So too with supervision: supervision exists to enhance the quality of the work you do. In doing so supervision concentrates on helping pastoral ministers to:

- Look after themselves: who is the 'I' doing the work, the person behind the professional minister?
- Remind themselves of what is needed to stay in good condition.
- Understand the brain and its impact on pastoral ministry, and especially the role of emotion and social connection in ministry.
- Make sense of pastoral ministry as an interactive process (always seeing it as a directive process).

How does supervision help? Two definitions capture for me the essence of what supervision does. According to Ryan:

Supervision interrupts practice. It wakes us up to what we are doing. When we are alive to what we are doing we wake up to what is, instead of falling asleep in the comfort stories of our clinical routines and daily practice. We have profound learning difficulties when it comes to being present to our own moment-to-moment experiences. Disturb the stuck narrative. The supervisory voice acts as an irritator interrupting repetitive stories (comfort stories) and facilitating the construction of new stories.[25]

According to Houston: 'Supervision is the creation of that free space where the supervisee lets herself tell back so that she hears herself afresh and invents in imagination how she can best be for her client in their next session.'[26]

The Experiential Learning Cycle is the theory of learning underpinning supervision. It involves four modes of learning (or knowing) moving from the present (doing the work) to the past (reflection on action) to the future (reflection for action).

In their presentation of the Experiential Learning Cycle as applied in the area of Coaching, Law et al[27] suggest three movements:

(1) An internal to external movement. The internal movement involves reflection and conceptualisation of new learning. This, in turn, leads to the second external movement from action/application of learning to new practice.

(2) A past, present and future movement: past experience is reflected on the present, which gives rise to new meaning which is then integrated into future work.

(3) A movement within changing meaning – the meaning and interpretation of our experience changes as we critically hold it up to examination.

Reflection is the key learning modality in supervision. Moving to experiential learning involves using reflection. Reflection and critical reflection learning involves supervisees in honest consideration and investigation of their work. Supervisors facilitate this reflection in order to help the supervisee learn from their own practice. With open mind and open heart and open will,[28] the supervisee is transparent, honest, aware and alert to what is happening as they reflect on the procedures, processes and relationships involved in the pastoral work they do.

With reflection we sit at the feet of our own experience.[29] We become students of our work. We learn from what we do. Reflection is not a given.[30] Many people live unreflective lives, which means, in effect, that they do not access the frontal cortex of their brains.[31]

Transformational (transform-actional) change and learning takes place when we let go of old ways of individual and collective thinking and behaviour that trap us. Langer[32] talks about 'premature cognitive commitments' – how easy it is to commit ourselves to beliefs without examination. The ugly duckling is a good example: its first premature cognitive commitment was that it was a duck, and its second, that it was ugly. It took time and experience for this hapless creature to realise it was neither of the commitments it had made. Our premature cognitive commitments trap us in categories that ensure we don't re-examine our values and beliefs and recommit to them. Scharmer[33] talks of three open stances that facilitate the movement between these forms of learning:

(1)   Open mind – what new truth will emerge.
(2)   Open heart – what new relationships will emerge.
(3)   Open will – what new action will come.

Supervision concentrates on how we learn and leads us through a number of learning stages.

LEARNING STAGE 1:
DOWNLOADING (FROM FEAR) – CLOSED MIND, CLOSED HEART, CLOSED WILL

Downloading is a form of learning where we hear what we want to hear; we project our old learning onto new learning; we sift through our existing models and frameworks. We listen, see and hear from within our own story. We make the new fit the old. With my fear and need to be secure, I do not recognise what I see, I do not say what I think and I do not do what I say. In safe certainty I keep fear at bay and I can easily take the moral high ground of being right, certain and having the truth. At worst, I am fundamentalist learning. I only hear what confirms my commitments, my certainties. Fine puts it well: 'Evidence that fits with our beliefs is quickly waved through the mental border control.'[34] Actually I am not a learner. Called 'I-in-me' learning, I recycle what I am committed to. Once you are certain you start downloading.

I find shaving a fascinating time for conversations with myself. I look in the mirror and there I am, looking back. I have heart-to-hearts with myself. One conversation I often hear myself having is undoubtedly a downloading conversation:

You are absolutely right about that.
How could he be so insensitive?
It is typically her – wrong again.

And as I shave I replay yesterday's conversation, and I find myself right again. I justify, I convince. I am right. Fundamentalist me.

LEARNING STAGE 2:
CURIOSITY AND DEBATING – OPEN MIND

This is 'I-in-it' learning. I move away from me, and I take another stance. I now debate. I wonder 'if'. What if I argue, discuss and allow other opinions, values, perspectives into awareness? I allow some disconfirmation of my thinking, my pet theories. I probably won't dispel entirely my 'best' ideas but at least I am open to other intellectual ways of thinking. For a time I get outside the prison of my own story and realise other stories exist. Much teaching is based on this form of intellectual exercise as we critique and debate the various possibilities. I had a good friend who was a master debater. He prided himself on arguing any side of the debate and was equally eloquent taking either. It was an intellectual game. As I shave I find myself saying to my reflection:

> Rehearse that argument with me again.
> And what if he says this?
> Ah, got you there – how do you respond to that?
> Give me the arguments for that again.

I marshal my arguments, I rehearse what I want to say, I destroy the opposition intellectually, and I smugly win again. Intellectual debater me.

LEARNING STAGE 3:
RELATIONSHIPS – OPEN HEART

A Sufi maxim says that, 'Fear knocked on the door. Love answered and there was no-one there.' Learning Stage 3 moves away from fear. The third stance is 'I-in-you' learning. We listen to ourselves reflectively and to others empathetically. Now I connect emotionally and have an open heart as well as an open mind. Can I begin to see it from others' perspectives? Speak to me. I am not buying your truth but I am certainly prepared to rent it. Empathetic learning allows us to leave the comfort of our own stories and join others' stories for a while. I interrupt my own stories, I leave my comfort zone, I am unsafe. I can now reflect – I have the ability to allow you and your thinking and your ideas and your values to be an open subject for me.

And in the mirror I hear me say to myself (the relationship is always with myself first and then with others):

What am I denying to myself?
What am I pretending not to know?
What am I hiding?
What feedback am I not giving to myself?
What conversation with myself am I avoiding?
What am I colluding with myself over?
What feelings am I not expressing?

I now live with psychological truth. Relationship me.

LEARNING STAGE 4:
COURAGE – OPEN WILL

The fourth stance is 'I-in-now' learning, transformational learning based on generative dialogue. How can we talk together in ways that change us all – can we listen from the perspective of the whole system? With generative dialogues, we co-create new realities together. 'In the field beyond right and wrong, I will meet you there' (Rumi). In the field beyond catholic and protestant, I will meet you there. In the field beyond tribalism, I will meet you there. In the field beyond competition, in the field beyond who is better, in the field beyond what the research says ... I will meet you there. In the field beyond whatever and wherever, I will meet you there. We will meet and, as someone said, camp out beside the questions for a while. We will stop talking and listen more. We will be open. We will be prepared to see our own prejudices and mindsets and mental maps that keep us where we are. We will see the thinking behind our thinking, the learning behind our learning. We will try to see the bigger picture. We will reflect, and reflect more and even more. And we will be courageous to go where the experience is taking us. I will see myself as part of the problem and part of the solution. We will let go of pet theories and well-worn dictates.

My talk with myself in the mirror takes on a different glow:

> What do you need to let go of in your way of thinking?
> What truth do you need to suspend?
> What are you afraid of?
> What vulnerability are you not facing up to?
> What loyalties does this bring to the fore?

Supervision must open and transparently examine and reflect on what is and what might be. I allow the voices in: the quiet, unspoken voices, the powerless voices, the underprivileged voices, the abused voices, the hurt voices. And in my supervision I ask:

> What voices need to be heard?
> What words need to be spoken?
> What truths need to be acknowledged?
> What connections need to be made?
> What assumptions need to be challenged?
> What beliefs need to be reviewed?
> What emotions need to be expressed?
> What actions need to be taken?
> What relationships need to be named?
> What secrets need to be uncovered?
> What strengths need to be seen?
> What limitations need to be articulated?
> What victories need to be celebrated?
> What losses need to be grieved?
> What mental maps need to surfaced?
> What is the shift that needs to be enabled?
> What fears am I not facing? (Self-transcending me.)

Transformational learning and supervision is about shifts in mentality:
- From the unexamined life to continual reflection (downloading has little reflection)

- From mindlessness to mindfulness
- From individual to communal
- From isolation to connectedness
- From sameness to surprises
- From static to developmental
- From head to heart and head
- From competition to cooperation
- From greed to generosity
- From denial to facing fear
- From authority to experience
- From teaching to learning
- From the what of learning to the how of learning to the process of learning
- From fear to courage.

CONCLUSION

Nelson Mandela was reported as saying in a speech: 'As we are liberated from our own fear, our presence automatically liberates others.' In supervision we begin to move away from fear and through the levels of learning, and our pastoral ministry moves with us. We move to transformational learning for ourselves and others.

It is quite a challenge to deal with the demands of modern living and the modern workplace both personally and professionally. We have to hold so much together: our own needs, those of our families and communities and the needs of others who are different to us. We face difficult times at work – demanding organisations, clients, co-workers and politics of the work environment. We face ominous futures, which include global warming, the energy crisis, fundamentalism and terrorism, not to mention banking and money recessional problems. Never were inner strength, staying power, confidence and optimism more needed. Never have we needed to look after ourselves more.

Martin Luther once said: 'I have so many things to do today: I better spend another hour praying.' Perhaps our version of that could be: 'I have so much to do, so many deadlines to meet, clients to look after, people to manage – I better spend another hour in supervision.' The last word will be left with R.D. Laing. He said, and kept saying, over and over again, what for me is the basis of transformational learning: 'There is nothing to be afraid of.'

QUESTIONS FOR REFLECTION

I.   What is the role of emotion in pastoral theology/ministry?
II.   How might insights from neuro-science (study of the brain) help pastoral ministry?
III. How can we set up forms of supervision that add value to pastoral ministry?

NOTES

1. C. Rogers, *A Way of Being*, Boston: Houghton Mifflin, 1995, p. 80.
2. J.C. Norcross and J.D. Guy, *Leaving it at the Office: A Guide to Psychotherapist Self-Care*, New York: Guildford Publications, 2007.
3. S.T. Covey, *The Seven Habits of Highly Effective People*, London: Simon and Schuster, 1989, p. 297.
4. T. Skovholt, *The Resilient Practitioner: Burnout Prevention and Self-Care Strategies for Counsellors, Therapists, Teachers and Health Professionals*, Needham Heights, Mass.: Allan and Bacon, 2001, ix.
5. M. Zuboff and J. Maxmin, *The Support Economy: Why Corporations Are Failing Individuals*, New York: Penguin, 2002.
6. Skovholt, op. cit.
7. C. Fine, *A Mind of its Own: How your Brain Distorts and Deceives*, Cambridge: Icon Books, 2007.
8. C.O. Scharmer, *Theory U: Leading from the Future as it Emerges*, Cambridge, Mass.: SOL Publications, 2007.
9. S. Jourard, *The Transparent Self*, New York: Van Nostrand Company, 1964.
10. D. Sirota, L. Mischkind and M. Meltzer, *The Enthusiastic Employee*, New Jersey: Wharton School Publishing, 2005.
11. M.D. Abrashoff, *It's Your Ship: Management Techniques from the Best Damn Ship in the Navy*, New York: Warner Books, 2002.
12. C. Tavris and E. Aronson, *Mistakes were Made (but not by me)*, Orlando: Florida: Narcourt Publications, 2007.

13. T. Lewis, F. Amini and R. Lannon, *A General Theory of Love*, New York: Vintage Books, 2000.

14. P. Ekman, *Emotions Revealed: Understanding Faces and Feelings*, London: Weidenfeld and Nicolson, 2003.

15. Lewis et al, op. cit., 2000.

16. S. Gerhardt, *Why Love Matters: How Affection Shapes a Baby's Brain*, Hove, East Sussex: Routledge, 2004.

17. D. Goleman, *Emotional Intelligence*, London: Bloomsbury Publishing, 1996.

18. J. Hughes and S. Youngson, *Personal Development and Clinical Psychology*, Chichester: Wiley, 2009.

19. William James in E. Langer, *Mindfulness*, Cambridge, Mass.: Perseus Books, 1989, p. 9.

20. *The Seven Habits of Highly Effective People*, op. cit., p. 21.

21. Cited in Covey, p. 22.

22. M. Wheatley, *Leadership and the New Science*, San Francisco: Berrett-Koehler, 1999.

23. R. Quinn, *Change the World: How Ordinary People can Accomplish Extraordinary Results*, San Francisco: Jossey-Bass, 2000, p. 24.

24. D. Mearns, *Person-Centred Counsellor Training*, London: Sage, 1997.

25. S. Ryan, *Vital Practice*, Portland, UK: Sea Change Publications, 2004.

26. G. Houston, *Supervision and Counselling*, London: Rochester Foundation, 1990.

27. H. Law, J. Ireland and Z. Hussain, *The Psychology of Coaching*, Mentoring and Learning, Wiley: Chichester, 2007.

28. Scharmer, op. cit.

29. L. Zachary, *The Mentor's Guide: Facilitating Effective Learning Relationships*, San Francisco: Jossey-Bass, 2000.

30. J. Moon, *Reflection in Learning and Professional Development*, London: Kogan Page, 1999.

31. M. Carroll and M. Gilbert, *On Becoming a Supervisee: Creating Learning Partnerships*, London: Vukani Publishing, 2005.

32. E. Langer, *Mindfulness,* Cambridge, Mass.: Perseus Books, 1989.

33. Scharmer, op. cit.

34. Fine, op. cit., p. 106.

LOOKING TO THE FUTURE

Bairbre de Búrca

WHO DO *YOU* SAY THAT I AM?
This is a perennial question, asked in every age, and answered in many ways. And still the question lives on, inviting engagement. The answers can unfold, sometimes by study, sometimes by prayerful dialogue with the sacred texts, sometimes by life experiences, sometimes by enlightenment, sometimes by wise leadership or example. Theological libraries are full of the fruits of insights that emerged from dialogue with the texts, with life situations, with the journey of coming to know who Jesus is. Despite the answers that have already been uncovered, and the truths that have already been revealed, this is very much a personal question to the individual as well as to the group, a question that still continues to demand attention. Sometimes the question is too difficult to wrestle with, sometimes too difficult to receive, sometimes so far away from any conscious desire or thought that it seems not to exist. Yet, for each of us, our changing life situations require that we examine the question afresh, again and again.

READING THE SIGNS OF THE TIMES
The conference selected the title 'Who Do You Say That I Am' as a way of opening a conversation about the mission and ministry of Jesus in today's world. This chapter is a continuation of that conversation. It probes the question at a seminal moment in history. On a global scale, with the world banking system collapsing, corrupt or incompetent governments experiencing resistance from hitherto supine citizens, climate change radically altering the environment, the breakdown of family life as a consequence of changing mores, it is clear that society, as it is

currently constituted, has many cracks and appears to be in a spiralling state of dissolution. In Ireland, the government is in disarray, power has been misused and trust has been abused. Greed has driven the economy into the ground. Society is fractured, with drugs becoming an ever-increasing problem. The power of the once dominant Catholic Church has weakened, and with that has come a loss of sustaining structures of meaning that once held communities together, albeit often far removed from the inclusive, compassionate and loving core values of the founder. Among the emerging signs of the times in post-modern Ireland, are as follows:

- Breakdown of traditional support systems, created by distance of commuter belts from extended family and workplace
- Inadequate health and educational services
- Increase in incidents of racist behaviour, often triggered by fear of work deprivation and scarcity of resources
- One-parent families, and the associated tensions of work/childcare/self-esteem/poverty
- Increasing prevalence of urbanisation, leading to loss of identity and disconnection with roots
- Disconnection with a core set of meaningful values, with not enough nourishment of the spirit or exposure to meaningful liturgies
- Climate change
- Breakdown in trust of authority and authority figures.

These are just some of the pressing issues in the turbulent milieu within which the pastoral minister is both living and serving. New situations lead one to question the old answers to 'who do *you* say that I am'? This leads to new conversations and exploration, and into a new learning cycle. The hope is that we can use this time of crisis as an opportunity to implement necessary change to structures and systems, and to look at how we are in relationship with each other and with the earth.

WHERE TO FROM HERE?

I do not pretend to have clear and tidy answers to this difficult question. However, the challenge is to look to the future, in conversation with the ideas formulated in the papers presented heretofore. Robert Kinast defines pastoral care as:

> ... a liberating, transformative response to persons in their life cycle development or at times of stress by an agent of the Church who uses primarily the resources of the person cared for as well as the resources of the Church to contribute to a fuller integration of the person with the community of faith and the community of faith with the person cared for.[1]

I am mindful that pastoral ministry is not confined to the professionals but is the call to all who are followers of Jesus. I am drawn to the servant model of pastoral ministry. I am also influenced by the experience of psychosynthesis, which construes the person as *relational*, unfolding to self and other in relationship; *dynamic*, the possibility of change and growth present; *complex*, with many layers of consciousness; and *unique,* with their own individual gifts, shadow and history. In my experience, engagement with another (in this case with the previous chapters) is a two-way process that takes place as one expands and is touched by the interaction with 'other'. There is also a confirmation of Self. Stimulated by the conference papers, I hope to reflect on both my encounters in my professional role as chaplain and my ordinary everyday encounters with the person of Jesus through the people I meet and who meet me. I will continue the conversations by attempting to weave together the rich threads gathered from the papers within a framework of dialogue with self, dialogue within families, dialogue within communities, dialogue with the threat to the Cosmos and dialogue with the Judeo-Christian tradition.

FIRST ESSENTIAL STEP: DIALOGUE WITH SELF

Clearly articulated through the different chapters, dialogue with self is essential as a foundational response. Before the question 'who do *you* say that I am' was addressed formally by the contributors, the conference opened with a focusing ritual. Using symbol, story, poetry, prayer, music and movement, the question was creatively opened out to include people from every walk of life. It subtly suggested that we use many masks to hide from the truth of who we really are. Through the use of a metaphorical story, the difficulties of really entering the world of the 'other' were illustrated graphically. This story was reminiscent of the promise in Isaiah that 'the lion will lie down with the lamb'. It illuminated the journey and challenges that need to be faced and endured before that promise might be a reality. Participants were drawn into a deep moment of personal reflection. In my moment, uppermost in my mind and heart was the imminent wedding of my youngest daughter. I noted how difficult it was, carrying the experience of excitement, anxiety and overload from family pressures, to attend to the question. I was, like Martha in the Gospel story, 'busy about many things' and not very well able to be attentive to a possible encounter. But then that is the common experience.

As already stated, the reality is that the task of being a pastoral minister is not confined to when one is 'in role', but also takes place informally in the ordinary events of life. How one embodies or meets the person of Jesus can happen in mundane moments, such as queuing at a checkout, sitting beside someone in a doctor's waiting room, wiping a child's runny nose, or in such wonderful happenings as delivering a new life into the world, listening to Haydn's 'Creation' symphony or seeing the radiant hope-filled, loving face of one's youngest on the happiest day of her life. The 'who do you say that I am' question is held in the on-going dance between ordinary and extra-ordinary everyday events along with the professional experiences. As Michael Carroll says, we are ministry-in-action, not functional ministers.

Attention to one's own inner processes is of the essence if one is to be open and receptive to dialogue with another, as Jesus was. But most of us experience many blocks in our capacity to be present to self. There are many and varied distracting experiences in our own lives that can consume our minds and energies. Karlfried Graf

Dürckheim[2] in his book *The Way of Transformation* guides his readers into spiritual practices in everyday life. These repetitive exercises enhance the capacity to become open and permeable to the Divine. He draws on insights from depth psychology, Christian mysticism and Zen. This book, which has recently been reprinted after being out of print for many years, may be helpful for those interested in learning how, in a practical way, to encourage growth in self-awareness and thus create a greater possibility of making connections with another. The beauty of this practice is that it utilises such ordinary activities as posting a letter by doing it mindfully, and it is a never-ending adventure.

Those who practice centring prayer, twice daily for twenty minutes, also find an increase in their capacity to sit with and listen to whatever is being spoken to them. Patience and receptivity grows, thus enhancing the capacity to minister to and be ministered to in return. The energy generated by belonging to a group who are practising meditative presence is very helpful and supportive to one's own practice. For example, some years ago I spent two weeks on retreat in a Buddhist monastery in Plum Village, France. The experience of living with the monks and sharing in their daily routines was extraordinarily enlivening as well as peace-inducing. Every time a bell or phone rang, everyone paused for the duration of three breaths, before continuing with whatever they were doing. The monk who was on phone duty had the chance to gather himself and to be fully present when after the third ring he picked up the phone and said 'Bonjour'. It was a long way from the present experience of having a mobile phone at hand, and minds constantly distracted from 'presence' to anything other than providing instant response to its unceasing clamouring. (In the Plum Village example the phone reverted to the role of instrument rather than that of controller.)

Healing dialogue happens when we are met, listened to and feel heard. Further wounding and damage to self-esteem can be inflicted when one is not listened to, not received as an equal, when the conversation does not get past the starting line. It is necessary to begin with oneself and one's own inner conversation, to realise truthfully what attitudes, prejudices and perceptions we might need to change if we are to be effective ministers or pastors to others. Change often happens slowly and imperceptibly, but it does happen when one individually commits to undergo the journey, the Way.

SECOND ESSENTIAL STEP: DIALOGUE WITHIN OUR FAMILIES

Pastoral ministers all belong to a family community. The family, like the Church, is a living system. As Anne Codd says, authentic community is inseparable from mission. No family today is untouched by some of the signs of the times referred to above. These provide countless opportunities to listen, to discuss, to encounter the different perceptions and to share 'the joy and hope, the grief and the anguish'[3] between men and women, young and old. The topics are endless. These include changing values, loneliness, religious understanding, fear of abandonment or of rejection if one doesn't match up. To engage with 'other' in this context is challenging at times. There is an inherent danger for the family member involved in ministry. One is often flown in to sort out family troubles, as if one had a magic solution to a problem that is often part of the very family system of which one is part as well. Being a pastoral presence in these situations can be difficult. It can be very challenging to accept that anything might be amiss in the family system. But there is also the possibility of growth, of change, of creating a new respectful understanding of difference.

Where an unmarried family member becomes pregnant, there is now a much more humane and Christian approach. It is rare that women are forced by the sham of respectability to give up their children for adoption, or to abandon their family of origin and go into hiding. Feelings can run deep between parents and their son or daughter. All that may have to be honoured before growth and reconciliation to the changing circumstances occurs. The State has recognised and long since given recognition to the status quo, providing an allowance and housing where necessary.

One related area, however, where there is not much sign of change and growth is the mystique of the perfect family and faith life which surrounds the First Communion event in families. For many blended or non-traditional families,[4] this can be a time of acute distraction from the wonder of the sacrament because of the complexity of family relationships today. Yet at times, it can also become a pastoral opportunity for healing, for reconciliation within the disparate relationships, and for a renewal of understanding of a compassionate God who loves all of us unconditionally. A healing encounter between a wise pastoral person, who listens, meets and affirms an articulate hurting woman is modelled in the stories of Jesus meeting the Samaritan woman and the woman caught in adultery. Both parties to the conversation were led to new understandings of each other's position. Timothy Radcliffe explains that Jesus' meeting with others starts with recognition, not blame, a good model of pastoral ministry in the setting of one's family.

As parent, family member, or in one's role as pastoral minister, the question of how to engage with someone struggling with being gay is coming more to the fore. Feelings of anger, hurt, shame, disappointment, discomfort, confusion, isolation, condemnation, abhorrence can surface. Many parents, partners, friends need help to enable them to accept the fact when it emerges. It is often an easier question to deal with in theory than in practice. As a pastoral presence, there is a responsibility to reflect and take ownership of one's own sexual identity in order to authentically help another on the same difficult journey of integration. In this regard, supervision, as so eloquently outlined by Carroll, is essential. We can't lead people into the freedom of Christ, attractively heralded by Radcliffe, unless we enter some of that freedom for ourselves.

The knotted question of sexuality has been dealt with by Church and by society in various ways throughout the centuries. None of the responses are perfect, and the challenge to find a truth that is many faceted and relevant to today's circumstances remains. Within families and society, where there is openness to the difficulties and complexities of human relationships, there is some chance of being helped to come to a deeper understanding of all that is involved.

There are many other challenges that impinge on family life at present, not least of which is work/life balance, how we care for the elderly, the sick and the vulnerable in our families. There are great possibilities for growth as well as burnout. At the heart of every family, pastoral care is provided daily as we minister to each other in the ordinary daily events of washing, working, cooking and loving. One of the life-changing events for me was seeing the way my neighbour bathed her profoundly handicapped daughter. Samantha was unable to do anything for herself, and as she got bigger, she got heavier and more awkward to manage. Despite the burden placed on the twenty-year-old mother, she had engaged and reflected on her situation. Seeing Samantha one day being lifted out of a bath, gathered in her mother's arms and wrapped lovingly in a towel, was like being present at a living pieta. It emerged in conversation that her mother had come to that understanding earlier. This had helped her in a mysterious and profound way to cope generously with the daily grind. She grew in her relationship with Jesus by becoming familiar with prayer and conversing with the gospel story. As she did so, resentment and self-pity at her lot had melted away. She handled her daughter with a reverence that was profound. This was real, not at all pious and it moved me deeply. It invited and attracted me to look again and connect to the story for myself. Not preaching but lived example was the key to begin my journey in faith. This echoes what Radcliffe said about pastoral care being a tiny bit of the conversation that is God.

THIRD ESSENTIAL STEP: DIALOGUE WITHIN OUR COMMUNITIES

The power of diversity in dialogue is the call to conversion. It compels us to become aware of our perceptions, to evaluate, to change, to become more open and often less definite. While this is the call to all, there is an added urgency for those working in formal pastoral ministry to model the kind of leadership-in-action which is reflective of the respect, the courage and the life-giving quality of Jesus.

Communities are made up of opportunities to care for the other, to encounter difference, to affirm and be affirmed. One can do that in a formal way as a pastoral minister, but also in the nitty gritty random encounters that call forth compassion, love, patience, or understanding of otherness. My experience, growing up on a main road in Glasnevin, was not one of belonging or connecting. Rather, we kept ourselves to ourselves. We had a veneer of respectability which had to be preserved at all times. It was typical of many households of that time, families that didn't have much but made the most of appearances. When I moved because of marriage out to a site situated at the foothills of the Dublin Mountains, I had few social skills for mixing with neighbours. As I was of the era when women had to leave work once married, I experienced extreme loneliness and isolation in the beginning. Luckily my husband had no such inhibitions, and neither did many of my new neighbours. I gradually overcame my reserve and was drawn into conversations and community despite my shyness. This led to wonderful exchanges over the years with diverse groups of people, and has been a very fruitful and nourishing place to finally 'grow up'. Our immediate neighbours were from the inner city, and knew none of my inhibitions. This taught me, slowly and painfully at times, to let go and to open up to difference.

There were some good summers back then and the circle widened to include the country people, an English woman, a German couple. Over cups of tea after a thirsty day in the garden we began our conversations, and without quite knowing what we were at, we slowly claimed our own diverse identities. It was affirming to name and speak our own stories and be heard, not judged. The father of the English woman had been a fireman in London during the Blitz, while the father of the German man had fought in both world wars. This had left a huge burden of guilt on his young son, and was part of the reason the couple ended up in Dublin. We allowed ourselves to be recognised, warts and all, by the other. It was a little like the power of the Icon, to which Radcliffe refers, where another looks at us and sees who we are. A process of deepening of self happened, and strong friendships were forged that still hold us in each other's hearts, despite the divergence of our paths since. This experience of dialogue and personal growth is not unique to my community, but happens in many places where communities grow together in respectful dialogue.

Today, life is not so simple. The diversity is greater, with language, culture and colour perceived as a barrier to belonging. The role, energy and calling power of priests has diminished greatly and there seems to be no definitive replacement. So the issues of inclusion/exclusion remain largely unaddressed. For example, the Travelling community are shunned by most sectors of society. There does not seem to be any meaningful dialogue happening in an attempt to come to meaningful resolution to meet the diverse needs of settled and Traveller people. The lion is not yet ready to lie with the lamb and a shift in understanding of both settled and Travelling people will be required before any progress on this thorny issue begins. This rejection is a real challenge to us as a Christian community.

In cities, unceasing traffic and a myriad of roads divide communities into different socio-economic groupings. The churches are half empty. Pastoral ministry in this context requires constant creative dialogue and response. Our community at parish level in Balally is actively working to create a space where conversations might begin. Visitation by lay parishioners, going two by two, has taken place in the past two years to the new residents of the high rise apartment blocks that have sprung up on every piece of spare land in the neighbourhood. The purpose is to welcome and to inform newly arrived people about the social services and social fabric of the area, the local clubs, schools, church communities of all denominations. An invitation is issued to all to gather publicly to meet leaders of all sorts of groups and clubs, including football and boxing clubs, drama groups, bereavement services, community Gardaí, church ministers and those at the Neighbourhood Family

Resource Centre. While this is slow work, it is about being a presence in the neighbourhoods and recognising the presence of the other, without distinction on grounds of race, class, creed or colour. The local SuperValu store has a multi-cultural staff. They engage daily with the multi-cultural clientele that makes up the neighbourhood. Children from very diverse cultural backgrounds are attending the local schools and 'inter-culturation' is taking place as children make new friends and their parents begin to interact.

The contemporary issues of the day are all present in microcosm within this community. To return to today's societal problems, there is a loss of identity, with locked gates on the high rise apartments, and little opportunity to meet newcomers naturally. One-parent families often live in isolation from their support systems. Many migrant workers live in isolation from any sort of social network. The challenge is to ensure that those who are not coping have access to the helping services. As Codd has affirmed, the search for human community goes on apace. Slowly people are inching their way into dialogue and subsequently settling into the new shape of our community. Creative things are happening in other communities too. For Thomas Grenham, the pastoral task is to discover and observe the manifestation of God's vision within every culture and religion. The opportunities for pastoral ministry are immense, and the demands are immense too. Care for self as outlined by Carroll will allow extra energy and creativity to flourish in the field.

FOURTH ESSENTIAL STEP: DIALOGUE WITH THE FUTURE OF THE EARTH

All thinking, rational people must by now be aware of the environmental dangers that lie ahead if as individuals and societies we do not take action on the very real and present problems besetting our earth. It will be a terrible legacy if, because of our inaction, we leave the next generations to sort out our mess, as they try to survive, to breathe, eat, live in a devastated world. There is a responsibility being thrust on all to engage personally in a dialogue with the earth and its goodness, with a view to passing it on intact to future generations. The water to be found in the land of the Maori people in New Zealand is held in trust for those who come after them. They are bound and committed to leaving these waters in a better condition than they received from their ancestors. They embody the fruits of whatever dialogue they have encountered with the Cosmos. As pastoral ministers, whether professional or working quietly alongside the people we meet, this could be a good example to inculcate in self and in other, to work towards conversion of habits of waste and carelessness. We need to grow in awareness, as pastors of the earth, of the interdependence of all living things in the Cosmos. Codd says that 'authentic pastoral ministry ... brings to consciousness and to action the deep relatedness of person, community and cosmos'. A group that actively helps in that field are the Eco-Church communities that are springing up around Ireland and Britain. They aim to encourage churches to celebrate the gift of God's creation, to recognise the interdependence of all creation, and to care for it through their life and mission and through members' personal lifestyles.[5]

FIFTH ESSENTIAL STEP: DIALOGUE WITH THE TRADITION

All these conversations can take place with or without connection to the tradition of Christianity. Indeed much is learned from people of other traditions and people of no professed denominational faith. But there is a body of teaching and of story in the gospels that awaits the searcher. The word was made flesh and dwelt amongst us and each year, religiously or irreligiously, we still acknowledge that event in the celebration of the Christmas season. For some, the knowledge that 'he comes, comes, ever comes' is alive. For others, the celebration is a material swirl of spending, giving and receiving gifts in love, without a personal knowledge of the founder of the feast. With the totems of our society in recent decades falling by the day, people generally are becoming more open to considering, revisiting, renewing and reshaping values that we live by. Now that the seduction of Mammon is being exposed for the sham that it is, people may be open to the possibility of true wealth being spiritual in nature rather than temporal. This is not to imply that poverty is good. Poverty and all that is associated with it is evil.

What needs to happen in the system of Church that will energise new engagement with the Word, the person, the mission and the ministry of Jesus? How can the Word be 'preached, broken, lived' in today's world? The example of the preacher Paul may be a lens through which to view and examine our ministry. Paul, after his conversion experience, took three years out before he re-emerged, preaching for Christ rather than against him. This would indicate that there may be need for a time of withdrawal, to wait for God to reveal a new way.

Certainly throughout the dioceses of Ireland, there is need for a period of grace to allow peace to settle after the ravages of the outcome of the report of the child sexual abuse disgrace. People need time to heal, anger to be received, betrayal to be forgiven. But they also need to realise that by the call of baptism, all are members of this flawed, yet potentially beautiful Church.

Now that we have the opportunities of life-long learning, it is possible to broaden long worn-out childish understandings, to begin to answer the question freshly, 'Who do you say that I am?' in dialogue with the sacred texts, in the context of the life and understandings we have today. For too many still operate out of a childish knowledge of the things of God, yet have many experiences in their adult lives which might help them connect more deeply. There is a fresh call to personal engagement in theological reflection, to ponder on an event in one's life and to see what might connect to it within the gospel story. It is probably best done in groups, where one articulates the problem to a wider wisdom, instead of being something that only happens in the small hours of the morning, when niggles and 'non-meeting' situations have a habit of pushing themselves up into consciousness. *Lectio Divina* is an ancient but timeless way to encourage people to engage with the Word that is in dialogue with daily living.

CONCLUSION

I have offered the reader a glimmer of an answer to the question, 'Who do *you* say that I am?' Powerful and meaningful liturgies may offer some connections to the answer as well. A beautiful ritual has the potential to bring into presence the nearness to the transcendent. Those of us involved in preparing and/or attending at daily liturgy, be it the repetitive chant of morning or evening prayer, or the simple daily action of Eucharist, will have experienced the possibility of a moment of meeting. When all involved have worked well together in preparation, when the liturgies are authentic and relevant to the time and place, and many of the gifts available to the community have been included, then something infinitely more than the sum of the parts is possible. Such liturgies are rich, nourishing, healing happenings. Too often, however, the community does not have an opportunity for co-responsibility, and that can shrink the actual sense of Divine Presence that is possible. All liturgies have the potential, as reiterated by Grenham, to help us construct life-giving meaning, and reflect the presence of God. But sometimes one's inner eye needs to be opened to see the possibilities and the connection that it has with our lives, but that, too often, we don't meet. A badly prepared liturgy is as painful at times as the non-meeting with a person. One can feel diminished, let down, even abandoned. Maybe it is time for lay people to step forward and take on the responsibility of learning more about what is possible, what gifts are available and how glorious liturgy is. As Codd says, there is an essential connection between ritual and life, Eucharist and community. There is a vast wealth of liturgies of the Word, which have mainly fallen into disuse. Good liturgy, when a body of people gather together as the people of God, to worship and to pray, provides a container wherein answers to the question, 'Who do *you* say that I am?' can unfold, astonish, nourish and heal.

Liturgy has the power and potential to bring Jesus to birth in us, to nourish his life in the community and in the individual, to give expression to the kingdom here on earth. The thirteenth-century Dominican mystic Meister Eckhart has the final word:

What good is it to me for the Creator to give birth to the Son if I do not also give birth to Him in my time and my culture? This, then, is the fullness of time when the Son of God is begotten in us.

NOTES

1. Robert L. Kinast, *Sacramental Pastoral Care*, New York: Pueblo Publishing Company 1988, p. 5.

2. Karlfried Graf Dürckheim, *The Way of Transformation, Daily Life as Spiritual Practice*, Sandpoint, ID: Morning Light Press, 2007.

3. *Gaudium et spes: Pastoral Constitution on the Church in the Modern World*, Vatican II: 1981 edition edited by Austin Flannery, OP, Dublin: Dominican Publications, 1980, p. 903.

4. See Finola Kennedy, 'Family Change in Ireland Over the Past Decade', *Child Links* (Spring/Summer), Dublin: Barnardos, 2004, for the increase in the diversity of family forms in Ireland.

5. Eco-Congregation is an ecumenical organisation. www.ecocongregationireland.org.